The Zoni English System

Writing Team: Sultan Stover
Mary Fierro

Methodology Team: Mary Fierro
Sultan Stover
Evina B. Torres
Zoilo C. Nieto

Editor: Evina B. Torres
Zoilo C. Nieto

Director: Zoilo C. Nieto
Evina B. Torres

ZONI ENGLISH SYSTEM
A Unique Classroom Instructional Method™

Zoni English System, DYNAMIC READING, Second Edition

Copyright © 2018, 2011 by Zoni Language Centers

All rights reserved. No part of this publication may be reproduced or transmitted in any form or by any means, electronic or mechanical, including photocopy, recording, or any information storage and retrieval system, without permission in writing from the publisher.

Requests for permission to make copies of any part of the work should be mailed to: Permissions Department, Zoni Language Centers, 22 W. 34th Street, New York, NY 10001.

Sales Department: U.S. and international: (212) 736-9000

Foreword

The Zoni English System has been designed as a classroom instructional method in response to the great need demonstrated by non-native speakers of English in their everyday lives in English-speaking countries.

Since communication is essential for survival, the Zoni English System method is based on daily life situations, while explaining fundamental expressions as well as grammatical structures. By doing, we have also utilized high-frequency vocabulary. Effective textual materials increase the student's motivation to continue studying English by influencing his or her attitude toward learning as well as enhancing his or her future possibilities.

OBJECTIVES

Zoni English System, Dynamic Reading features student-centered lessons that enhance reading and writing skills of the students. The book provides human interest stories rich with vocabulary words and reading comprehension exercises. It provides activities to improve reading skills such as scanning for main ideas, skimming for details, and making predictions. Topics for discussion include world topics such as diversity, family, alternative medicine, happiness, and consumerism. Writing is introduced through journal writing, paraphrasing, summarizing, and personal story writing. A variety of creative and proven methodologies and strategies are implemented to enrich the learning and teaching experience, therefore achieving the Zoni English System objectives.

TO THE TEACHER

In the classroom
Teacher talking time 20% - 30%
Student talking time 70% - 80%

Methodology and Techniques To Be Employed:
Instructors utilize such teaching techniques as:

- Ask & exchange
- Backward build-up drill
- Chain drill
- CIP (Choral Intonation Practice)
- Cloze exercise/fill in the blanks
- Concept-checking questions
- Contextualization
- Cooperative learning
- Conversation practice
- Debate
- Demonstration
- Dialogue practice
- Dictation
- Direct method
- Elicitation
- Elicitation through inference
- Error-correction
- Expansion/Drawing out activities
- Group work
- Horseshoe
- Hot seat
- Inferential questions
- Interactive reading
- Information gap
- Internet research
- Jigsaw
- Listen & repeat
- Multiple pair practice
- Multiple slot substitution
- Matching
- Open-ended story/Round robin story
- Pair work
- Party time
- Peer correction
- Positive suggestion
- Project: individual/group
- Q & A (Question & Answer)
- Reading & listening
- Realia
- Role play
- Self-correction
- Sentence completion/transformation
- SPPD (Structure-Practice-Presentation-Dictation)
- Stand up activity
- Structure feedback
- Substitution drill

Teachers who have not gone through the Zoni co-teaching program are required to follow the methodology and techniques detailed in the **Zoni Teacher's Manual**.

Important Symbols:

Teachers consult the **Zoni Teacher's Manual** for instructions.

Teachers assign individual or group projects after each unit to assess students' knowledge of the language skills.

Teachers make groups of two students for Pair Practice.

Zoni English System, Dynamic Reading emphasizes reading and writing using cooperative learning that facilitates group work and student centered classroom activities. This increased importance placed on student-centered learning in the Zoni classroom supports the enhanced and simultaneous usage of all four language skills. Each student is given greater amounts of class time to practice the target language, thereby maximizing student learning and progress in the classroom.

Classroom Seating Arrangements

In addition to applying various teaching methodologies, teachers are also encouraged to vary their classroom seating arrangements based on the lesson. The number of students and class size are factors that will also help to determine the seating arrangements.

Standard

This type of seating arrangement, where students are arranged in rows, is generally used for lecture-type lessons and presentations. It is also beneficial when we need all the students to be focused on a particular task on the board. Students are able to work at their own pace while doing their assignments. It tends to be teacher-centered. The teacher must circulate and make lots of eye contact with his/her students to ensure all are involved in the assigned task.

In the Zoni System, lessons generally begin with the standard seating arrangement, especially during the introduction of a grammar point.

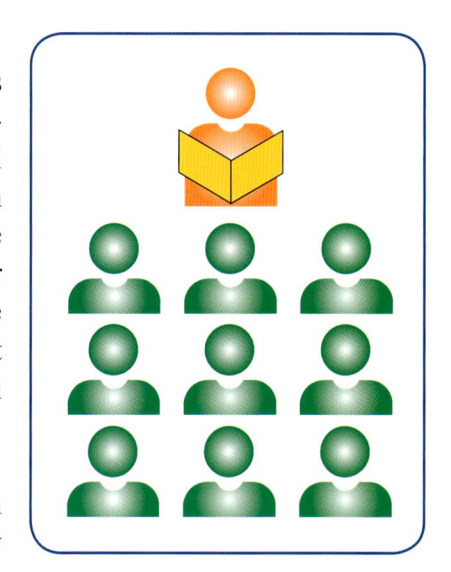

Semi-Circle

This seating arrangement is recommended when maximum student interaction is required to focus on a particular task, such as getting information from the board or audio-visual activities and exercises. Students are able to see their classmates' gestures and facial expressions easily during discussions. In addition, it is less teacher-centered, so it provides lots of student interaction.

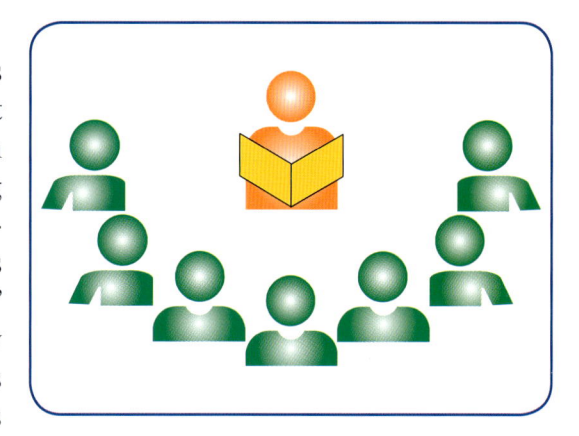

Circle: Group Work

Group work generally consists of three or more students, is designed for maximum student participation. Students are more relaxed about experimenting with the language and the fear of making mistakes is diminished. Group work is a cooperative learning experience where students learn from one another. Group work becomes very effective when the groups are given clear instructions, tasks related to the objective of the lesson, and a specific allotment of time in which to complete the assigned tasks.

Pair Work

Pair Work has the same conditions as group work but with two students.

In the lower and intermediate levels, the Zoni System incorporates a lot of group work and/or pair work during the practice period sessions.

Homework

When we assign homework to students, it is important that we also check it in the following class. Checking homework should not take more than 15 minutes. Make sure you check all students' homework, but vary your homework-checking routine; for example, check it in the second hour of class. Finally, keep a record of which students have not done their homework. For each assignment not completed, a student gets a zero. Alert any student who receives a lot of homework zeroes, as he or she may have to repeat the course.

SURPRISE FACTOR
Though developing a routine in the classroom is good, at other times, it is critical that teachers change their classroom routines to keep students on their toes.
Some ways to use the surprise factor are:

1. Checking the homework in the second hour of the class period instead of at the beginning of the class period.

2. Asking the class a question, then zeroing in and calling on a student to answer it.

INDISPENSABLE ORAL PRACTICE
The Zoni English System encourages choral and individual repetition in order to improve the students' pronunciation and to help them lose any fear of the language. Teachers should not be reluctant to practice pronunciation even with upper-level students; all students of any level benefit from this frequent practice. Teachers should also ensure that students keep their books closed and do not take notes during the introduction of a new subject or during oral practice. Their focus must remain on the task and subject matter.

ELICITATION FROM THE STUDENTS
Take advantage of students' prior knowledge by eliciting vocabulary and examples from them. By doing so, we share their knowledge with the rest of the class, build confidence, promote active thinking, and stimulate students to come up with interesting examples.

BOARD WORK

At Zoni, we believe in keeping board work as simple as possible, especially when teaching the beginner and intermediate levels. Board work is beneficial in that teachers can use it as a resource for student practice when doing Choral Intonation Practice (CIP), drilling and role playing. Board work keeps students focused. Board work reinforces reading and spelling.

While doing board work, make sure all students have their books and notebooks closed. No writing or copying is allowed during this period. All students must be focused on the board. Write in print, not cursive. Plan what you will be putting on the board ahead of time. If writing a long dialogue, work your dialogue one segment at a time. We strongly recommend that teachers follow our board work examples displayed in the **Zoni Teacher's Manual**.

ATTENDANCE

Learning English is a matter of constant and consistent practice and dedication. Student attendance is vital for maximum learning and benefit; this is why teachers must remind students that regular attendance is necessary. If students do not comply, they may be asked to take the course again. Attendance should not be taken for granted. Encouragement and reminders about class attendance are essential.

ACKNOWLEDGMENTS

We are very pleased and proud to announce the publication of a new book in the Zoni English System series: *Zoni English System, Dynamic Reading*. The experience of constantly challenging the status quo has led to the creation of this book. Many people have been involved in this project; their passion, persistence, dedication, and teamwork made it possible to complete *Zoni English System, Dynamic Reading*. We would like to thank **Masami Soeda** for her exceptional graphic design work that consistently enhances the Zoni teaching and learning experience. We would also like to thank **Danielle Belisle**, **Laura Di Domenico**, **Charles Heil**, **Melissa Hillie**, **Sharon Itkoff**, **Max E. Sanchez**, **John David Zurschmiede**, **Victoria Ochoa** and **Miyuki Adachi** for their valuable input. We very much appreciate the cooperation and suggestions of the Zoni faculty. In addition, we would like to recognize the contributions of Zoni students who have provided us with much-needed feedback.

Zoilo C. Nieto & Evina B. Torres
Directors

TABLE OF CONTENTS

UNIT 1 — DIVERSITY

LESSON 1 Describing Celebrations — PAGE 2
Fourth of July & Thanksgiving
Celebrating Golden Week and Fourth of July

LESSON 2 Describing a Place — PAGE 10
Country Life
City Living
Living Conditions in NYC
Living in Vancouver, Canada

LESSON 3 Describing a Person — PAGE 27
Michael Jordan
Angelina Jolie

LESSON 4 What is Diversity? — PAGE 33
What is Diversity?

UNIT 2 — FAMILY

LESSON 5 What is Family? — PAGE 44
The Evolving Concept of Family

LESSON 6 Stories of Love and Marriage — PAGE 52
How They Met

LESSON 7 Family Journeys — PAGE 62
My Great-Grandparents and Their Journey

LESSON 8 Immigration — PAGE 71
Will It All Stay the Same?

UNIT 3 — ALTERNATIVE MEDICINE

LESSON 9 Being Healthy — PAGE 84
Alternative Medicine

LESSON 10 Finding Out the Facts — PAGE 96
Acupuncture's Popularity on the Rise in the West

LESSON 11	Interviewing an Expert	PAGE 114

A Doctor's Opinion on Alternative Medicine
ER (Emergency Room)

UNIT 4 — IN PURSUIT OF HAPPINESS

LESSON 12	What Is Happiness?	PAGE 136

The Pursuit of Happiness

LESSON 13	What Makes You Happy?	PAGE 148

The Triumphant Story of Carmen

LESSON 14	Home Is Where the Heart Is	PAGE 159

Nobody Loves Buddy

LESSON 15	Don't Worry, Be Happy	PAGE 169

Guess Who's Depressed?

UNIT 5 — CONSUMERISM

LESSON 16	What Is Consumerism?	PAGE 182

What Is Consumerism?
What is the Price of a Karaoke Machine?

LESSON 17	Comparing Opinions	PAGE 198

Zoni Radio

LESSON 18	Public Opinion Surveys: What do consumers want?	PAGE 211

Survey on Smartphones

FINAL ORAL EXAM — PAGE 223

Dear Zoni Student

We would like to welcome you to **Zoni English System, Dynamic Reading**. In order to get the most out of your study of English, you should always do the following:

- Speak only English in class.
- Attend class every day.
- Do all assigned homework.
- Read all the stories and passages.
- **Relax and have fun!**

UNIT 1

DIVERSITY

Got Respect?

> "We cannot change if we don't survive, but we cannot survive if we don't change."
>
> —Anonymous

Info tip:
In the year 1995, 48 percent of all foreign-born residents in the United States came from Mexico.
What is your prediction for this year?

Source: US Bureau of the Census

Lesson 1: Describing Celebrations

Fourth of July

The Fourth of July is a national holiday that celebrates the birth of the United States of America as an independent nation, separate from the kingdom of Great Britain. Every year on July 4th, Americans celebrate the signing of the Declaration of Independence by lighting fireworks and having parades, barbecues, carnivals, fairs, picnics, concerts, and various other public and private events that celebrate the history, government, and traditions of the United States.

Thanksgiving

Thanksgiving is an American and Canadian holiday celebrating harvests and family. In the United States, Thanksgiving is traditionally celebrated on the fourth Thursday in November, while in Canada, Thanksgiving is celebrated on the second Monday in October. It is a day when families get together and share a large traditional meal with typical foods such as turkey, cranberry sauce,

A Pilgrim Thanksgiving

Discussion Questions

GROUP WORK: Jigsaw

Work in groups. Imagine what celebration is taking place in these pictures. Then discuss the following questions with your group and share your group's answers with the other groups in the class.

1. Who are these people?

2. What are they celebrating?

3. What do you think they are saying to each other?

4. What do you think they did to prepare for the celebration?

5. Have you ever participated in a Fourth of July or Thanksgiving Day celebration?

6. Do you have similar celebrations in your country? What are they?

7. How do you prepare for these celebrations?

8. Why is it important to have national celebrations?

9. How are celebrations in your country similar to or different from the celebrations in the United States?

Journal Writing

A. Many people keep journals about ideas, feelings, and reactions to the events in their lives. In this class you will be encouraged to keep a journal of your reactions to questions and situations that your teacher will give you. Your first journal topic is about a celebration that takes place in your country. Write about it and refer to the questions:

- √ What is the celebration?
- √ When does it take place?
- √ What does it commemorate?
- √ How do you celebrate it?
- √ What preparations do you make?
- √ Why is it important?

MY JOURNAL

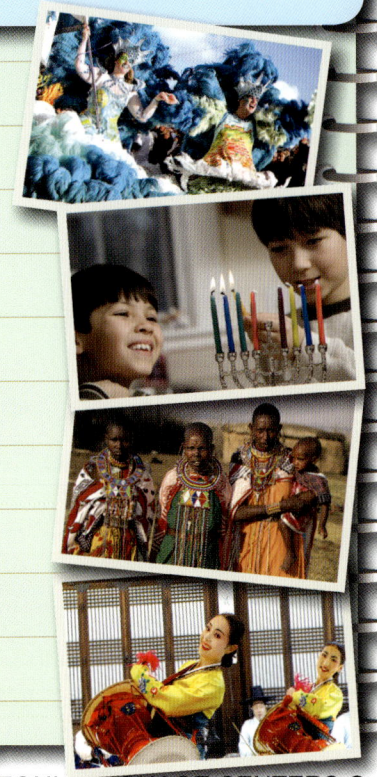

B. PAIR WORK

Exchange journals with a partner. Read your partner's journal. Then write a response to your partner's journal in the space provided below. (Example: Think of a similar celebration in your country and describe how it is different.) Remember: You will be reacting to a very personal experience, so try to keep your comments honest, but positive.

COMMENTS ON MY PARTNER'S RESPONSE

_____
_____
_____

Conversation Practice

A. Read with your group to find the definitions for the boldfaced words and put a one-word synonym in the box. Use contextual clues to understand the meaning of the words.

CELEBRATING GOLDEN WEEK AND FOURTH OF JULY

Maggie: Good morning, Junsuke.

Junsuke: Hey, Maggie. How are you?

Maggie: I'm okay. Are you **excited** about the party tonight?

Junsuke: I don't know if I'll be able to go. My family is celebrating Golden Week tonight, and I have to **participate**. It's a family tradition.

Maggie: Oh, I'm so sorry you can't come. I thought your family had been here in the USA for a long time. By the way, what is Golden Week?

Junsuke: Yes, my grandmother came here thirty years ago, but we still celebrate some of the Japanese holidays. Golden Week is a Japanese holiday celebrating Children's Day, the birth of one of our national leaders, and our constitution.

Maggie: Oh! It's like the Fourth of July here in the United States.

Junsuke: Kind of. How do you celebrate July 4th?

Maggie: Well, there are fireworks and my family has a barbecue in the park. We spend it together with our friends. There are a lot of *festivities*[1] in the city also. It's all to celebrate America's independence from the British.

Junsuke: It sounds like Golden Week, except we don't really have a barbecue outside.

Maggie: Actually, the barbecue is one of the best parts of July 4th. I can already imagine the *aroma*[2] of food cooking on the grill. It's also really fun in *metropolitan*[3] cities like New York and Miami. There's a *massive*[4] celebration, including fireworks, music, and picnics.

Junsuke: That's cool. I'm *accustomed*[5] to seeing fireworks for Golden Week. What else happens?

Maggie: The holiday is really *diverse*[6]. Every city does different things. People usually *congregate*[7] to watch the fireworks together, and the streets are *packed*[8] with people. It's like a big party.

Junsuke: I can't wait to experience the Fourth of July.

Maggie: Me neither.

Junsuke: Maggie, do you want to come with me to my grandmother's house to celebrate Golden Week with us?

Maggie: Sure! And you know it would only be *courteous*[9] if I invited you to my family's house on the Fourth of July.

Junsuke: Okay. I'll call you later.

Maggie: I'll be ready. See you later.

Synonyms

1. _____
2. _____
3. _____
4. _____
5. _____
6. _____
7. _____
8. _____
9. _____

COMPREHENSION QUESTIONS

1. What are Junsuke and Maggie talking about?
2. Why can't Junsuke go to the party with Maggie?
3. How long has Junsuke's family lived in the United States?
4. How do people celebrate Golden Week? How do you know?
5. What does Maggie offer Junsuke?

B. MATCHING

Match the words in column A with their meanings in column B. Identify the part of speech according to how the words are used in context. The parts of speech are: noun, adjective, verb, and adverb.

COLUMN A			COLUMN B
1. massive	d	adjective	a. gather together in one place
2. aroma			b. many different kinds of things or people
3. crowded			c. happy party or celebration
4. packed			d. huge in size or amount
5. magical			e. polite, having good manners
6. congregate			f. large city which is the center of some activity
7. accustomed			g. good smell, usually of food
8. diverse			h. many people in one place
9. metropolitan			i. surprising or amazing
10. courteous			j. used to
11. festivities			k. too many people in a small space

Sentence Completion

Complete the summary by using the correct form of the words in the box below.

WORD BOX

crowd	magic	congregation
festive		
courteously	accustom	metropolitan

In large ¹_____ cities, people often feel lonely when they are not ²_____ to the place and people around them. Cities are often ³_____, but just because there are a lot of people around doesn't mean that a newcomer won't feel lonely. One way to become comfortable in a new place is to get involved in the celebrations and ⁴_____ that are taking place within one's own neighborhood. Often, people will ⁵_____ on the street during a celebration and a newcomer can easily go up to them and ask what is going on. Especially if the people are nice and ⁶_____, they will be happy to explain their customs. Big cities can seem confusing places but sometimes they can be ⁷_____.

Pair Work

With your partner, discuss your favorite holiday in the United States. Explain how it is celebrated, why it is celebrated, who the people involved in the preparations are, what unique customs and traditions are practiced, and how you feel about it.

Writing Activity

Write a dialogue about a holiday experience you have had since you came to the United States or Canada. Be ready to perform in class.

Lesson 2 — Describing a Place

NYC

BEIJING

Pre-Reading Activity

Group Work

Work in groups of three to discuss the pictures and answer the following questions.

1. How big do you think the two apartments in the picture are?

2. What is the main difference between the two apartments?

3. Which apartment is your current apartment more similar to?

4. Which apartment seems more comfortable?

5. Compare the apartment you live in now to your home in your native country? Which one do you prefer? Why?

Reading Exercise

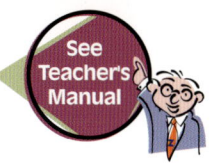

A. PAIR WORK

Partner A reads passage 1 and partner B answers the questions on page 12. Then switch roles. Partner B reads passage 2 and partner A answers the questions on page 15.

PASSAGE 1

Country Life

The house that I grew up in was *cozy* and just big enough for my family—my father, mother, and brother. It was an old house that had *character* and personality. The house was at the end of a tree-lined block, in a neighborhood where no one locked their doors at night because we knew everyone in the community. *Bordered* with a white picket fence, our house had a two-acre green lawn that *glowed* deep emerald green in the spring and summer. Behind my house was a big corn field that in the winter was the *grazing* home to a hundred black Angus cows. My brother and I would spend countless hours in a tree house that was *propped* onto the large oak tree in the center of our backyard. The tree was so *grand* that I would imagine it being there before anyone had set foot on the land before. My mother had a small herb garden next to our house and under my bedroom window. On hot summer nights I would open the window and breathe in the natural *aroma* of the clover and jasmine that my mother had planted. We had two dogs and they ran freely in the fenced yard. The dogs would bark and chase any car that would drive by. That was not very often because our nearest neighbors lived three miles down the street. No matter how much noise my brother would make, the dogs and I would have no one to complain to about it. In the winter the trees lost their leaves, the grass died, and everything became gray and cold. Every Saturday morning my father would spend hours chopping firewood that he had **retrieved** from the nearby forest. At the same time, my brother and I would be in the kitchen helping my mother make pancakes or waffles, depending on whose turn it was to choose. I **preferred** pancakes but my brother preferred waffles. I would go ice fishing in the local rivers that would freeze over due to the **incredibly** cold temperatures in the winter. I never caught anything, but it was a good excuse to go out and **commune** with nature in the wintertime.

B. Comprehension Questions

1. What does the author mean when he says that the house had personality?

2. Did they live in a bad neighborhood? Why or why not?

3. What herbs from the herb garden could the author smell?

4. How many dogs did they have?

5. What does "chop firewood" mean?

6. Why would the rivers freeze over?

7. What other activities can one do when he or she communes with nature?

C. VOCABULARY IN CONTEXT

Read the sentences below and use contextual clues to write your best understanding of the boldfaced words.

1. The house that I grew up in was *cozy* and just big enough for my family.

   _____

2. It was an old house that had *character* and personality.

   _____

3. Our house had a two-acre green lawn that *glowed* deep emerald green in the spring and summer.

   _____

4. *Bordered* with a white picket fence, our house had a two-acre green lawn that glowed deep emerald green in the spring and summer.

   _____

5. Tree house that was *propped* onto the large oak tree in the center of our backyard.

   _____

6. The tree was so *grand* that I would imagine it being there before anyone had set foot on the land before.

   _____

7. On hot summer nights I would open the window and breathe in the natural *aroma* of the clover and jasmine that my mother had planted.

   _____

8. Every Saturday morning, my father would spend hours chopping firewood that he had *retrieved* from the nearby forest.

   _____

9. I *preferred* pancakes but my brother would rather have waffles for breakfast.

   _____

10. I would go ice fishing in the local rivers that would freeze over due to the *incredibly* cold temperatures in the winter.

    _____

PASSAGE 2

City Living

Since I came here three years ago, I have lived in a variety of diverse neighborhoods. Despite the differences between the areas and the people who live there, one quality remains *constant* in all: the noise. The city is so busy all day and night that it is hard to find a peaceful place to relax. Right now, I live on the second floor in a four-*story* building and my windows *face* Main Street. The *view* from my window doesn't *look out onto* trees with birds *nesting* in them, or onto green fields. Instead, I see brick houses, shops, cars, ambulances, and garbage trucks race up and down the street every day and night. People *congregate* on corners, drinking coffee and talking. It's a big difference from my hometown. In my town, people would never eat or drink anything in public. They also speak in quieter tones. This is one of the biggest differences between life in my hometown and life in the city.

People in this city are also so busy **making a living** that they barely have time to say hello to each other. I do not know any of my neighbors. Sometimes if I **recognize** someone from my building and they recognize me as well, they will **nod** quickly as they keep walking down the block. Back in my town, people greet each other courteously as they pass one another in the hallway or on the street.

However, there are some other big differences that are actually positive. For example, everything here is much bigger. The market here is the size of three or four shops at home. The market on the corner of my street **takes up** the whole corner of the block. I can buy all my groceries and necessities in one place. I save a lot of time shopping at one market rather than going around from store to store. There are very few small markets that are privately owned. Life is really different here. Oftentimes, I miss my hometown and the quiet there.

D. Comprehension Questions

1. How long has the author lived in the new city?
2. What is the writer's chief complaint about his or her neighborhood?
3. Does he or she complain about anything else? If so, explain.
4. What does the author like about his or her neighborhood?
5. How do you think the writer feels about where he or she lives overall?

E. VOCABULARY IN CONTEXT

Read the sentences below and use contextual clues to write your best understanding of the boldfaced words.

1. The noise is **constant** in my neighborhood. It does not stop for a minute.

2. I live in a seven-**story** house. There are seven floors in my building.

3. The front windows of my apartment **face** Main Street.

4. The **view** from my apartment is beautiful. I can see the ocean.

5. The birds in the trees near my house **nest** in the upper branches. They have built a nest, and that is where they will lay their eggs.

6. People **congregate** on corners, drinking coffee and talking.

7. I **make a living** as a nurse. That is how I earn money to live.

8. I do not **recognize** that person. I do not think I have ever seen him before.

9. If you do not know someone but still want to be polite, you can just **nod** your head to say hello.

_____

10. The store **takes up** the entire corner. There is no more room for any other building.

_____

Journal Writing

A. Write about your neighborhood. Describe a view from your window. Draw a map of the neighborhood. What do you see across the street, down the block, or just outside your window?

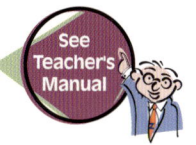

MY NEIGHBORHOOD

B. PAIR WORK - STUDENT A
  Read your neighborhood description out loud to student B.

C. PAIR WORK - STUDENT B: Listening Activity

Listen to your partner's description of his or her neighborhood and draw a picture of what it looks like. Write the adjectives or describing words/phrases that you have heard, or draw a picture of what you think it looks like. Then, reverse roles.

MY PARTNER'S NEIGHBORHOOD

Bonus Reading Activity

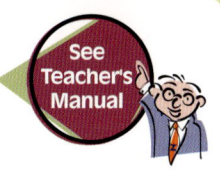

A. PAIR WORK

Read the passage below in pairs and answer the comprehension questions.

READING A

LIVING CONDITIONS IN NYC

Living conditions in New York City are notorious for being very expensive, very small, and inconvenient. For the price of owning a studio apartment in New York City, you could live in a luxurious five-room mansion in other parts of the United States. There are five boroughs where you can live in New York City: Queens, Staten Island, The Bronx, Manhattan, and Brooklyn.

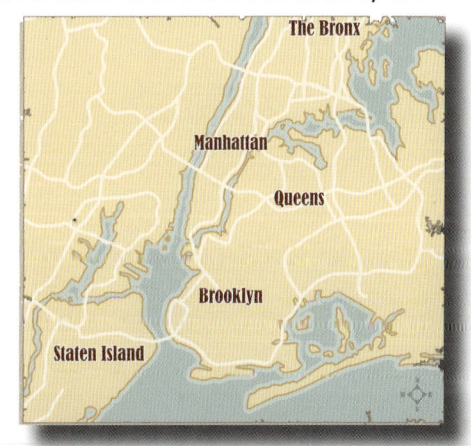

All of these places have different things to offer. In Queens, the most diverse borough of New York City, there are large enclaves of Spanish, Brazilian, and Greek cultures, creating a wonderful atmosphere of diversity everywhere you go. Staten Island is a community that is quiet and homey. It is an island that has a very scenic commute with views of the Statue of Liberty if you travel back and forth on a ferry to Manhattan. The Bronx is a diverse community that is the home to both rich and poor New Yorkers. Manhattan has grand architecture and busy streets, and people come here from all over the world to have an experience that cannot be found anyplace else. Brooklyn is the most populated borough in New York City, with more than 2.5 million people living together. (2017 US Census)

Each borough is unique and offers a special living opportunity to students and tourists. You can have a lot of different experiences in the city. Whether you are an F1* or non-F1 student, there are also a few different housing options available to you.

* F1 student: visa student pursuing a full course of study in the United States.

B. COMPREHENSION QUESTIONS

1. What is New York City notorious for?

2. What are the five boroughs of New York?

3. Which borough is the most diverse?

4. How can you get to Staten Island?

5. What kinds of New Yorkers live in the Bronx?

READING B

LIVING IN VANCOUVER, CANADA

Vancouver, Canada, is one of the world's most beautiful and interesting cities to live and study in. It is the largest city in the province of British

Columbia and one of Canada's most diverse. It is located on the Pacific Ocean, which makes it an important port for Canada's economy. Because the weather is moderate in both winter and summer, Vancouver is considered one of the best places to visit if you are interested in year-round sporting events. There is a lot of nightlife and many extracurricular activities to see and enjoy. In fact, Vancouver is considered a prime tourist attraction with a growing visual and performing arts scene. Compared to other large metropolitan cities in the world, Vancouver is considered one of the cleanest.

The economy of Vancouver is vibrant and expanding. There are a lot of businesses that make Vancouver their home base of operations in Canada. Vancouver has managed to attract many large businesses and innovative international companies that are looking to expand into Canada because of its large port and easy access to major destinations in Asia and the west coast of the Americas. Vancouver is also home to some of the best universities in Canada and attracts large numbers of students from all over the world.

Living in Canada can be very expensive. In fact, Vancouver is considered the most expensive city in Canada to live in. Renting a home, apartment, or condominium is the cheapest option. The government is working on ways to lower the cost of living in Vancouver, but so far its policies have been ineffective in doing so.

Vancouver is a city that is both beautiful and interesting because of its natural beauty and its bustling economy. It is also one of Canada's most diverse cities, making it a great destination for tourists, students, and businesspeople.

C. COMPREHENSION QUESTIONS

1. In which province of Canada is Vancouver located?

2. Why is Vancouver a good place to visit if you like year-round sporting events?

3. Why would businesspeople be interested in opening a business in Vancouver?

4. What is the most affordable living option in Vancouver?

5. Has the government made living in Vancouver cheaper?

HOUSING OPTIONS

These are the four housing options for most students that have come to the United States and Canada to study English.

Homestay:

When you live in a homestay, you are living in a room of someone's home, specifically with an American or Canadian family. You will be allowed to partake in family activities and meals if you choose to. This option is a great way to participate and understand the local culture, and practice your English with native speakers.

Shared Apartment:

In a shared apartment, you are renting a room in an apartment that you are sharing with others. You are not renting the entire apartment for yourself. You might have other roommates who are living there with you or you could be living with the owner.

Residence Hall:

When you live in a residence hall, you can have a choice of single, double, or triple occupancy in a room. Female and male rooms are separated. This type of accommodation is intended for students who will be sharing dorms with other students. There are amenities situated in common areas, which are shared by everyone.

Renting:

When you want to live on your own or choose who your roommates will be, you can rent an apartment. When you rent an apartment, you must be ready to take on all the responsibilities of a lessee, including the signing of a lease contract that is binding and legal pertaining to local rental laws. Also you have to pay a security deposit, which may be equivalent to one to two months' rent. You will be responsible for all damages to the apartment when you leave.

D. DISCUSSION QUESTIONS

1. Which New York City borough or Canadian city would you like to live in? Why?

2. Which living arrangement sounds best for you?

3. How much would you pay to rent an apartment in your city, in New York City, or in Vancouver?

4. What kind of apartment would you want? Describe your choice.

5. What do you think is a reasonable budget for you, for the following types of accommodations: homestay, shared apartment, residence hall, and renting?

6. Explain how you came up with these prices. How did you decide on this budget?

7. Describe your present living conditions. Where do you live and with whom?

8. Are you satisfied with your accommodations? Explain why or why not.

9. As a student, what part of your living setup is helpful to you?

10. When you visit other countries which type of accommodations do you usually stay in: homestay, shared apartment, residence hall, rented apartment, or other? Why?

E. PAIR WORK - LET'S TALK

Discuss with your partner the good and bad features of an apartment. You can use your imagination or talk about an apartment you have lived in. If you find the same answers, circle them.

GOOD THINGS ABOUT MY APARTMENT	BAD THINGS ABOUT MY APARTMENT
1. good location	1. small size
2.	2.
3.	3.
4.	4.
5.	5.
6.	6.
7.	7.

Writing Activity
WRITING A LETTER OF COMPLAINT

Many times we encounter problems with our apartments, and it can be difficult to deal with landlords because there are differences between what we expect from landlords in our new country and what we expected from landlords in our former country. The apartments that we find in these new places are also very different from what we had before.

Writing a formal letter is an important skill. In this unit you will write a letter of complaint. You can write a letter of complaint to your cable operator, phone company, landlord, and so on.

SAMPLE LETTER

Following the model, write your own letter in the space provided.

Sample

_____
Your Name

_____
Your Street Address

_____
City, State Zip Code

_____
Your Email

_____
Your Phone Number

Date _____
         Landlord's Name

Dear Landlord's name:

My name is _____
                        Your Name
and I am currently a resident in your building at
_____.
               Address
I have lived in your building for
_____. I
Length of Time Spent Living in the Apartment
am writing to tell you about
_____.
         Name of Problem

_____.
Brief Description of the Problem

Thank you very much for your time and attention to this problem. I hope that it will be resolved soon.

Sincerely,

_____
Your Signature

_____
Your Name in Print

Lesson 3 — DESCRIBING A PERSON

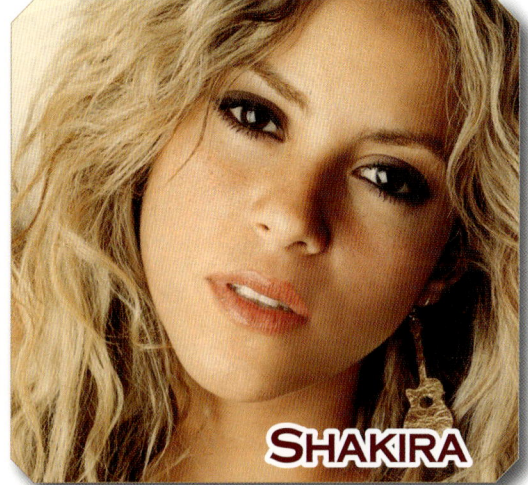

DAVID BECKHAM

SHAKIRA

Pre-Reading Activity

PAIR PRACTICE

PAIR WORK
Work with a partner and describe the pictures. Write five more questions about the pictures above. Then ask your partner.

1. Do you know these people?

2. Can you guess where they are from?

3. _____

4. _____

5. _____

6. _____

7. _____

Reading Exercise

A. PAIR WORK
Read the passage below in pairs and answer the comprehension questions.

READING A

MICHAEL JORDAN

Michael Jordan is **a modern-day success story**. He is one of the most recognizable sports figures in the world. He is also one of the most successful businessmen. Jordan grew up in a small town in North Carolina. As an African American, he had a difficult life growing up. Many people said he would not be successful in his life. His mother and father always encouraged him to do his best and to always **follow his dreams**. He grew up playing all types of sports. His favorite sport, believe it or not, was baseball. He began playing basketball in elementary school, and all of his coaches always said **he had a great gift**.

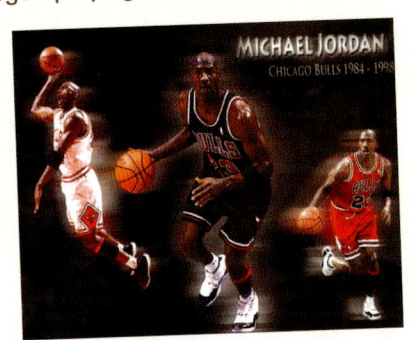

In college he played basketball for the University of North Carolina, and in the last game of the championship, he made the final winning shot. This was an amazing **boost of confidence** for Jordan and a **prelude** of great things to come.

He was soon drafted by the Chicago Bulls basketball team. At the time, the Chicago Bulls were the worst team in the National Basketball Association (NBA). After seven years of playing for the Bulls, Jordan helped his team win the NBA championship. It was a great moment for Michael Jordan. He always believed that he could achieve anything he wanted if he followed his dreams.

B. COMPREHENSION QUESTIONS

1. What was Michael Jordan's favorite sport growing up?
2. What sport is Jordan famous for playing?
3. Where did he grow up?
4. What college did he attend?
5. What gave Jordan a boost in confidence?

Bonus Question: What brand of sneakers did Michael Jordan make popular?

C. VOCABULARY BUILDING

Write the meaning of the following expressions and use them in a sentence to show you understand the meaning of the vocabulary from the reading.

1. **modern-day success story:** _____

2. **to follow one's dreams:** _____

3. **to have a great gift:** _____

4. **boost of confidence:** _____

5. **prelude of (great) things to come:** _____

READING B

Angelina Jolie

Angelina Jolie was born to be a superstar. She is one of the most talked about and beloved **American icons** of her generation—not only because of her acting but also because of her personal life, which has attracted so much attention. She has starred in many films and has become a **household name** all over the world for her **philanthropic** and humanitarian work. She is the daughter of famous American character actor Jon Voight.

Before she turned her attention to acting, Angelina Jolie wanted to become a funeral director. However, she quickly changed her mind after her first **brush with fame** as the girl in music videos for artists like the Rolling Stones and Lenny Kravitz. After a number of roles in a few smaller films, Jolie played a sociopath in the movie *Girl, Interrupted* and won an Oscar for the role. She went on to achieve international fame with her role as Lara Croft in the *Tomb Raider* films.

During the time that Jolie was filming *Tomb Raider*, she was also becoming famous for her wild and often strange personal life. She has tattoos all over her body. At one point, she was known to carry knives and walk around with a necklace full of blood. She was in constant fights with her estranged father, and she married Billy Bob Thorton, an actor much older than her. This was a very tumultuous time in her life, as reflected in the choices she made regarding her professional and personal life. She struggled during this period but was eventually able to move on from her wild and crazy past. Jolie met Brad Pitt on the set of their movie *Mr. and Mrs. Smith*. Pitt and Jolie had adopted three children and had three children of their own. What was once a very happy family ended in a bitter separation.

Although famous for her acting, Angelina Jolie is also considered one of the world's greatest faces for humanitarian causes, including the fair treatment of children. Because of this humanitarian work, Jolie has been given many awards and honors, including the United Nations Goodwill Ambassador award. It is hard to distinguish whether Angelina Jolie is more famous for her acting achievements, her personal life, or her humanitarian work. But one thing is for sure: she is one of the most recognizable faces on the planet, and as long as she can, she will continue to use her **star power** for good causes.

D. COMPREHENSION QUESTIONS

1. Who is Angelina Jolie's father?
2. What movie role made Angelina Jolie internationally famous?
3. How many children has she adopted?
4. For what movie did she win an Oscar award?
5. What is one award Angelina Jolie has received for her humanitarian work?

E. VOCABULARY BUILDING
Write the meaning of the following vocabulary words and use them in a sentence.

1. **American icon:** _____

   _____

2. **star power:** _____

   _____

3. **philanthropic:** _____

   _____

4. **a household name:** _____

   _____

5. **brush with fame:** _____

   _____

F. DISCOVERING THE TOPIC SENTENCE

The topic sentence is the main idea. To figure out the topic sentence of a paragraph, you may ask yourself, "What is the paragraph about?" or "Why is the author telling this story?" or "What's the writer's attitude or idea about the topic?" For example, the topic sentence of the paragraph is about how hardworking Michael Jordan is. You know that is the main idea because all of the details in the paragraph support that idea.

1. What is the main idea of the first passage about Michael Jordan?

   a. Michael Jordan was disappointed that he did not become a baseball player.

   b. Michael Jordan was unsuccessful at basketball.

   c. Michael Jordan was successful because of his determination.

2. What is the main idea of the second passage about Angelina Jolie?

   a. Angelina Jolie is one of the world's most famous people.

   b. Angelina Jolie became famous for her wild and strange personal life.

   c. Angelina Jolie became famous because of her acting.

Writing Activity
WRITING AN AUTOBIOGRAPHY

An autobiography is a personal narrative of someone's own life. For this task, you should write your own autobiography. Think of your life up to now. How would you describe yourself? For example, would you say that you are a hard worker? Then, give examples to illustrate your description of yourself. Write 2–3 paragraphs describing yourself and the highlights of your life.

Lesson 4 — What is Diversity?

Pre-Reading Activity

Discuss the following questions in groups of three. Share your opinions in class.

1. What does diversity mean to you?

2. Is diversity good or bad? Why?

3. What are some examples of diversity?

4. Describe a time when you experienced "culture shock" and explain how you dealt with it.

5. Have you ever inadvertently offended someone and their culture in the past? How did you smooth things over?

Reading Exercise

A. GROUP WORK

Read with your group to find the definitions for the boldfaced words and put a one-word synonym in the box. Use contextual clues to understand the meaning of the words.

WHAT IS DIVERSITY?

The word diversity has a simple meaning; on the most basic level it means difference. In the context of culture, diversity reflects the difference between various cultures' racial, ethnic, and religious identities. Each culture is unique in its own way, and as a result, diversity can be seen everywhere. Just on the **crowded**[1] streets of New York and Vancouver, we can see people from all over the world rushing **to and fro**,[2] taking the same subways, working and shopping together, and eating international food in crowded restaurants. Cultural diversity truly defines these international cities where **congregations**[3] of people of all ethnic and racial backgrounds live together.

When cultures collide, as they do in New York and Vancouver, our perceptions of the world, other people, and their belief systems, are challenged. If we live in isolation from other cultures, we are **accustomed**[4] to our own beliefs and ideas about the world. But in places that are diverse, we are forced to see other people's cultural, racial, and ethnic differences. This is both the beauty and difficulty of living in these cities because it is not always easy to be **courteous**[5] to people whose customs you find offensive. In fact, experiencing the cultural diversity in these cities, we can see that there is no one **universal**[6] truth; instead there are many truths.

Even within cultures, there are distinct differences that **manifest**[7] themselves within that particular culture. The United States of America and Canada are "melting pots" of different people from many different cultures in their largest cities, but much of the North American countries are also very **homogeneous**[8] in that Americans and Canadians live in separate communities and do not come into contact with many different people and cultures. A person from Utah might have very different beliefs and ideas from someone who lives in New York. A citizen of Canada living in Vancouver does not necessarily take part in the same festivities as someone from Saskatoon. This is also an expression of diversity.

We may not always realize or agree with how diversity affects people. We must understand that diversity is all around us. However, an overwhelming number of citizens welcome diversity and can sometimes challenge those in the extreme of the spectrum who do not accept it as a strength of the country. We are becoming more dependent on each other whether we wish to or not.

Have you ever felt discriminated against?

Synonyms

1. _____
2. _____
3. _____
4. _____
5. _____
6. _____
7. _____
8. _____

B. DISCOVERING THE MAIN IDEA

Check the line next to the sentence that expresses the main idea of the first two paragraphs.

1. In the first paragraph the author's opinion of diversity is that

    a: ☐ diversity is important to society.

    b: ☐ diversity has a very simple meaning.

    c: ☐ diversity can be seen in people's culture.

2. In the second paragraph, the author's main idea is:

    a: ☐ Cultural diversity can be seen in the differences among people from different countries as well as in the differences among people from different states.

    b: ☐ Crowded places are culturally diverse.

    c: ☐ Most people are surprised by diversity.

3. Write the main idea of paragraph 3.

_____

4. What specific cultural differences have you experienced among people from different countries?

_____

C. WRITING A SUMMARY

Summarize what the author of the article has said about diversity in one paragraph, in the space provide below.

See Teacher's Manual

D. VOCABULARY EXERCISE

Choose the correct meaning of the word and then use the vocabulary word in a sentence.

1. accustomed to

    a. used to   **b.** forget   **c.** take away

2. to and fro (idiom)

    a. happy thoughts   **b.** travel back and forth   **c.** good

3. packed
    a. full, with little room   **b.** itchy   **c.** bad thoughts

4. congregate
    a. walk around   **b.** group together   **c.** thinking

5. courteous
    a. polite   **b.** old   **c.** impossible

6. universal
    a. word of mouth   **b.** competent   **c.** believed by everyone

7. manifest
    a. last place   **b.** to appear or become understood
    c. a long road

8. homogeneous
    a. good feeling   **b.** marked by sameness
    c. a large body of water

Assessment

Project — See Teacher's Manual

Culture

Conduct Internet research on some famous Americans/Canadians who built the nation and contributed to its culture and diversity. Then write a five-paragraph essay describing the person. Include information on where he or she was from, what he or she did, and what made him or her famous. Cite your sources of information and avoid plagiarism.

Be ready to give a presentation in class.

GRAMMAR REVIEW

Simple Present and Simple Past Tenses

SIMPLE PRESENT

AFFIRMATIVE

> **Subject** + simple present form of the verb

NEGATIVE

> **Subject** + do/does not/don't/doesn't + simple form of the verb

QUESTION

> Do/Does + **Subject** + base form of the verb

    Meaning: routines, habits, facts
    Context Clue: every day, week, month, year; all the time; always

SIMPLE PAST

AFFIRMATIVE

> **Subject** + past form of the verb

NEGATIVE

> **Subject** + did not/didn't + base form of the verb

QUESTION

> Did + **Subject** + base form of the verb

    Meaning: finished events in the past
    Context Clue: yesterday; last week, month, year; the last time

Glossary

Vocabulary Word	Part of Speech	Pronunciation	Meaning
accustomed	adjective	[*uh*-**kuhs**-t*uh*md]	become used to
American icon	idiom	[*uh*-**mer**-i-k*uh* n] [**ahy**-kon]	held up as an ideal in America, often a famous person
aroma	noun	[*uh*-**roh**-m*uh*]	good smell of something, often food cooking
boost of confidence	idiom	[**boost**] [uhv] [**kon**-fi-d*uh* ns]	increase one's self image
border	noun	[**bawr**-der]	used to separate two different things
brush with fame	idiom	[**bruhsh**][**with**][**feym**]	first encounter with being famous
character	noun	[**kar**-ik-ter]	distinct or strong personality
chase	verb	[**cheys**]	follow
commune with	verb	[k*uh*-**myoon**] [wi*th*]	to communicate with, be close to (as in nature)
congregate	verb	[**kong**-gri-geyt]	gather together
congregation	noun	[kong-gri-**gey**-sh*uh*]	a group that gathers together usually for religious services
constant	adjective	[**kon**-st*uh* nt]	continual
countless	adjective	[**kount**-lis]	too many to be counted
courteous	adjective	[**kur**-tee-*uh* s]	polite
cozy	adjective	[**koh**-zee]	comfortable
crowded	adjective	[**krou**-did]	filled with people in the same place
descent	noun	[dih-**sent**]	coming from an ancestor
diverse	adjective	[dih-**vurs**]	different from one another
face	verb	[**feys**]	to deal with a problem; to look in the direction of
festivities	noun	[fe-**stiv**-i-teez]	party; celebration
follow one's dreams	idiom	[**fol**-oh] [**wuhnz**] [**dreemz**]	try to achieve one's goals
glow	verb	[**gloh**]	shine with intense heat or brightness
grand	adjective	[**grand**]	large, great, important
graze	verb	[**greyz**]	to eat grass or bushes
have a great gift	idiom	[**hav**] [*uh*] [**greyt**] [**gift**]	to have or possess a special talent
homogeneous	adjective	[hoh-m*uh*-**jee**-nee-*uh* s]	of the same or similar kind
household name	idiom	[**hous**-hohld] [**neym**]	well-known; common name that everyone knows

incredible	adjective	[in-**kred**-uh-buh l]	amazing, extraordinary
look out onto	idiom	[loo k] [out] [**on**-too]	when a window is facing a certain direction or an object, it is said to have a view of something; look in the direction of something
modern-day success story	idiom	[**mod**-ern] [dey] [suh k-**ses**] [**stawr**-ee]	a famous example of someone who has been successful and is still living
magical	adjective	[**maj**-i-kuh l]	supernatural or a feeling of amazement
make a living	idiom	[meyk] [uh] [**liv**-ing]	earn money to support oneself
manifest	verb	[**man**-uh-fest]	become seen or understood
massive	adjective	[**mas**-iv]	huge
metropolitan	adjective	[me-truh-**pol**-i-tn]	describes a large, diverse city
nest	noun/verb	[nest]	a place where birds lay their eggs made of sticks
nod	verb	[nod]	to move one's head up and down in agreement or recognition
packed	adjective	[pakt]	very close together in a confined area
perseverance	noun	[pur-suh-**veer**-uh ns]	to continue doing something in spite of difficulties
philanthropic	adjective	[fil-an-thropic]	the habit of giving
prefer	verb	[pri-**fur**]	to like one thing better than another
prelude	noun	[**prey**-lood]	an introduction to something, one thing that comes before another; sign of something to come in the future
prop	verb	[prop]	to support by placing one thing under another
recognize	verb	[**rek**-uh g-nahyz]	(verb) realize that you know someone or something
reflect	verb	[ri-**flekt**]	to show, to think deeply about
retrieve	verb	[ri-**treev**]	to take back
star power	idiom	[stahr **pou**-er]	the power of a celebrity to influence people
story	noun	[**stawr**-ee]	a short narrative; the floors in a house or apartment building
take up	phrasal verb	[teyk uhp]	start learning something new; occupy space
to and fro	idiom	[too en fro]	back and forth; here and there
universal	adjective	[yoo-nuh-**vur**-suh l]	something that is believed by everyone
view	noun	[vyoo]	(noun) the range of vision, (verb) to look at something

Source: Dictionary.com

UNIT 2

FAMILY

Family First

"The strength of the nation derives from the integrity of the home."
—Confucius

Info tip:
In the United States, reports show that 50 percent of marriages are projected to end in divorce. (www.divorcerate.org)

Why do you think this is happening?

Lesson 5 — What is Family?

Stand-Up Activity: Interview

Ask your classmates the following questions. Take notes of their responses and share them in class.

1. What is the typical size of a family in your country?

2. How involved are grandparents, aunts, uncles, and cousins in raising children?

3. Are there different codes of behavior required of male children and female children?

4. Would you like to have a family of your own someday? If so, how many children would you like to have?

5. Can you have a family by having an adopted child?

6. What is your concept of an ideal family? Why?

Journal Writing

A. Write about your family and refer to the questions.

MY JOURNAL

- √ Where are you from?
- √ How long you have been in the United States?
- √ How many members are there in your family?
- √ Who are they?
- √ What roles do they have as members of the family?
- √ How are important decisions made in the family?
- √ Who makes decisions?
- √ Have there been any changes in your family since you came to the United States?

B. PAIR WORK

Exchange journals with a partner. Read your partner's journal and write a response to what your partner has written. Is it similar in any way to what you have written? How is it similar? Are there many differences between what you have written and what your partner has written?

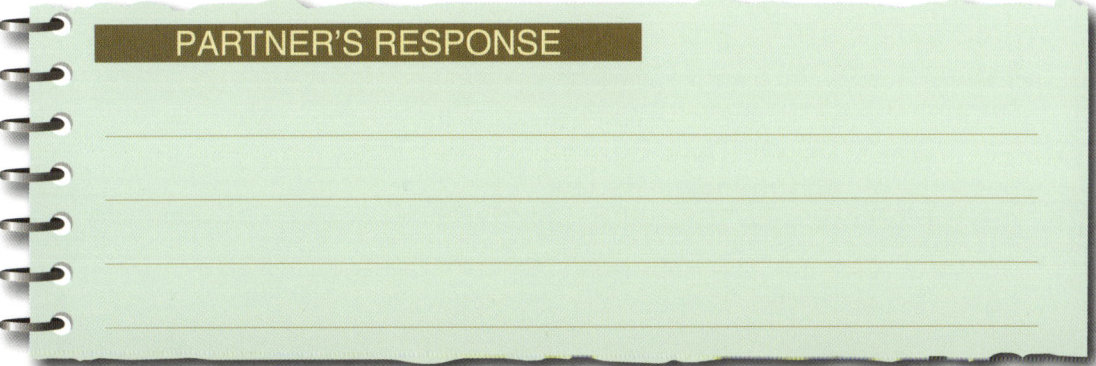

PARTNER'S RESPONSE

Reading Exercise

A. GROUP WORK:
Read with your group to find the definitions for the boldfaced words and put a one-word synonym in the box. Use contextual clues to understand the meaning of the words.

The Evolving Concept of Family

The **concept**[1] of family is a **universal**[2] one. Across time and culture, families have been the **foundation**[3] of society. However, just as the idea of family exists everywhere, the shape and **function**[4] of the family varies among cultures. The jobs individual family members perform can vary in different ethnic groups, cultures, religions, and historic periods. All of these factors can add to the meaning of family.

The **nuclear**[5] family is the modern idea that a family consists of a husband, wife, and children. This structure may be the **conventional**[6] view of a family today in the United States, Canada, and Europe; however, this **archetype**[7] is being challenged in many ways. Single-parent households are a **prime example**[8] of a new type of family. In fact, according to the 2009 US census, 26 percent of all children in the United States are being raised by only one parent. In the past, being a single parent

Synonyms

1. _____
2. _____
3. _____
4. _____
5. _____
6. _____
7. _____
8. _____

was *taboo*⁹, but because it has become a common sight in the United States, it is now accepted.

9. _____
10. _____
11. _____
12. _____
13. _____

In other countries, the word "family" goes well past the immediate relatives of the nuclear family and includes grandparents, aunts, uncles, and cousins. This is called the *extended*¹⁰ family. In some cases, it is not uncommon for a grandparent or aunt and uncle to be directly involved in the family unit, *raising*¹¹ and caring for the children; providing the home for husband, wife, and children; and even helping out with the finances of the family. Additionally, the customs of a culture affect where and with whom the family lives. For example, in the traditional family unit of the Bemba tribe of northern Zambia, Africa, the husband must move into his wife's village and family of origin's home once they are married. In South Korea, traditionally the eldest son moves into his parents' house with his new wife.

The family is the foundation of all human society. There may be differences in the *outward*¹² appearance of the family unit in different cultures, but the *underlying*¹³ function remains the same.

B. PAIR WORK: Comprehension Questions

In pairs, discuss the comprehension questions below and answer them in complete sentences.

1. What is the typical structure of a family in the United States, Canada, and Europe today?

2. What has changed in this family structure?

3. Typically, who are the members of an extended family?

4. What different jobs do members of the extended family often perform?

5. What two examples does the author use to show how a family functions in different countries?

C. MATCHING

Match the words in column A with their meanings in column B. Identify the part of speech (noun, adjective, etc.).

COLUMN A	COLUMN B
1. concept — noun	a. how something looks; surface; physical
2. universal	b. family made up of parents and children only
3. foundation	c. accepted by all as true or acceptable
4. function	d. best or first example of something
5. nuclear family	e. family made up of parents, children, grandparents, aunts, uncles, and so on
6. conventional	f. purpose; how something works
7. archetype	g. nurture; taking care of family and bringing up children

8. prime example   _____ _____
9. taboo
10. extended family   _____ _____
11. raising a family   _____ _____
12. outward appearance   _____ _____
13. underlying   _____ _____

h. hidden; not obvious, but true and basic
i. structure that holds up society
j. model
k. something forbidden by society; something not socially acceptable
l. idea
m. usual or typical; old-fashioned

DISCOVERING DETAILS

Details support the main idea of a paragraph. They may include any or all of the following points: reasons, which are explanations of the main idea; facts, which provide proof of the reasons; examples, which provide details of the main idea; and scenarios, which provide a possible situation to further support your main idea.

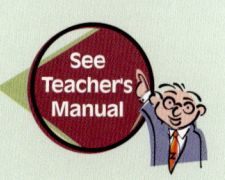

See Teacher's Manual

D. PRACTICE

1. Look at the second paragraph on page 46. Then check the main idea from the choices below.

   _____ The typical structure of the family is changing in the United States, Canada, and Europe.

   _____ The nuclear family is now made up of single parents and children.

   _____ Single parents are the majority in the United States, Canada, and Europe.

2. Now write two details found in the passage that support the main idea.

_____

_____

Writing Activity

A. Write three paragraphs about a typical family in your country. Include a main idea in each paragraph. Support your main idea with details.

> **Paragraph I**
>
> Describe the typical family structure in your country.

_____
_____
_____
_____

> **Paragraph II**
>
> How has the family structure changed in the past ten years?

_____

Paragraph III

How do you feel about the importance of family?

B. PRESENTATION

Read your composition in class, for intonation and pronunciation practice.

Lesson 6: Stories of Love and Marriage

Pre-Reading Activity

GROUP WORK: Jigsaw
Work in groups. Discuss the following questions with your group and share your group's answers with the other groups in the class.

See Teacher's Manual

1. What is the typical age at which a man gets married? A woman?

2. Where do people usually meet their love interests in your country? (church, parties, school)

3. Do people have arranged marriages in your country?

4. How long are people typically engaged before getting married?

5. Do people usually have religious, civil, or both ceremonies when they get married?

6. If you are married, how did you meet your spouse?

Journal Writing

A. Write about a married couple that you know. It could be friends, relatives or even you and your spouse. Refer to the questions to help you. Use new vocabulary words to practice.

MY JOURNAL

> √ Who is this couple?
> √ How do you know them?
> √ How did they meet?
> √ How long have they been together?
> √ What future plans do they have for their lives?

B. PAIR WORK

Exchange journals with a partner. Read your partner's journal and write a response to what your partner has written. (Example: Is it similar in any way to what you have written? How is it similar? Are there many differences between what you have written and what your partner has written?).

PARTNER'S RESPONSE

Reading Exercise

A. GROUP WORK:

Read with your group to find the definitions for the boldfaced words and put a one-word synonym in the box. Use contextual clues to understand the meaning of the words.

How They Met

1. My parents met while traveling on the Trans-Siberian railroad from Beijing, China, to Moscow, Russia. At the time, my father, who is an American, was a **civil engineer**[1] and was traveling to Moscow to help in the construction of a bridge near the capital. He had been in China working for an architectural firm that had developed large **humanitarian**[2] projects all over Asia and Europe, building roads, hospitals, and schools in areas where they were needed. My mother was an **exchange**[3] student from North Carolina living in China, and was taking a vacation from her studies to travel around Europe and Asia by train. My father was given the wrong seat on the train and ended up sitting next to my mother the whole trip. My mother was happy to meet someone who spoke English after a year of living in China with very little **access**[4] to people who spoke English.

2. They spent the next six days traveling and talking together. When the trip was over, they said good-bye and exchanged phone numbers and addresses, but went on their separate ways. Three years later, in New York, they met each other again by chance at the party of a **mutual friend**[5].

Synonyms

1. _____
2. _____
3. _____
4. _____
5. _____

It was the most **fortunate**[6] of accidents. They never expected to see each other again, but when they saw each other, it was as if they had not been apart for three years. They started talking and enjoying themselves as though they had been together for all that time. After that night, they dated for three years and then got married. They were starting a life together that had begun on that train ride. Was it **love at first sight**[7]?

6. _____
7. _____
8. _____
9. _____
10. _____
11. _____

3. For the next five years, they lived in New York, but when my mother became pregnant for the first time, they decided to move to North Carolina and live closer to her family. My father quickly found a job at a local construction firm and my mother found work as a teacher. They settled into their new lives and had four children: my brother Johan, my sister Emily, my younger brother Tim, and me. They worked hard to provide the best they could for us, and they always put family first.

4. After we had all graduated from college, my parents sold their home and moved to Florida. Now my mother **volunteers**[8] at an orphanage and helps **abandoned**[9] children, and my father is content playing golf every day. My parents have a yearly family reunion where all of us siblings go to Florida and visit them. My mother usually enjoys cooking for all of us just once a day, and the rest of the time we order out since she is just not used to cooking for a lot of people nowadays. My parents seem to have a very **cozy**[10] existence and their life has been full of excitement and **disappointment**[11], but they have managed to stay together. It may look like a simple thing, but these days it is a big accomplishment.

B. PAIR WORK: Comprehension Questions

In pairs, discuss the comprehension questions below and answer them in complete sentences using the adverb clauses in parentheses.

1. When did the author's parents meet? (while)

   The author's parents met *while* they were traveling on the Trans-Siberian railroad.

2. Why was the author's mother happy to meet someone who spoke English? (since)

3. How many days did they spend together after they had met on the train? (after)

4. How long was it before they saw each other again? (after)

5. How long did they date before getting married? (before)

6. How long had they known each other when they got married? (by the time)

_____

_____

7. When did they move to North Carolina? (after)

_____

_____

8. What have they done in their private lives since they retired? (since)

_____

_____

9. What do these parents do with their children when they visit Florida? (every time)

_____

_____

10. Does the mother still enjoy cooking for everyone? (since)

_____

_____

C. GROUP WORK: Discovering Main Ideas and Details

In groups of three, discuss the main ideas and details from the essay "How They Met" on pages 54-55. Then check the main ideas and write the supporting details for each paragraph based on the text.

1. Look at the first paragraph. Then check the main idea of the paragraph.

_____ My parents liked each other immediately.
_____ My parents met by accident.
_____ My parents like to travel.

Write one or two details that support the main idea.

_____
_____

2. Look at the second paragraph. Check the main idea of the paragraph.

_____ My parents had a lot of friends in common.
_____ My parents never expected to see each other again.
_____ My parents wanted to get married.

Write two details that support the main idea.

_____
_____

3. Look at paragraph 3. Write the main idea on the lines below.

_____
_____

Write two details that support the main idea.

_____
_____

4. Look at paragraph 4. Write the main idea on the lines below.

_____

_____

Write two details that support the main idea.

_____

_____

D. VOCABULARY IN CONTEXT

Read the sentences below and use contextual clues to guess the meaning of the words.

1. After going to school to study to be a ***civil engineer***, my father worked on many projects building bridges and roads.

civil engineer: _____

2. The Red Cross operates all around the world doing ***humanitarian work***, especially in areas that have been affected by natural disasters or wars. It serves people in need.

humanitarian work: _____

3. I lost a lot of money when I traveled to Europe because the ***exchange*** rate was very high.

exchange: _____

4. My mother was happy to meet someone who spoke English after a year of living in China with very little ***access*** to people who spoke English.

access: _____

5. Both of us knew Susie. That was how we met each other. She was our *mutual friend*.

mutual friend: _____

6. After the earthquake, many people from all over the world *volunteered* to help out those affected by the disaster.

volunteered: _____

7. They never expected to see each other again, but the next time they met, they went on to date for three years and got married. Was it *love at first sight*?

love at first sight: _____

8. After their car ran out of gas, they had to *abandon* it on the side of the road and walk to the nearest town.

abandon: _____

9. My parents have a yearly family *reunion* gathering, where all of us siblings go to Florida and visit them.

reunion: _____

10. Their house was very *cozy*. They were very comfortable living there.

cozy: _____

11. Although they experienced many *disappointments* in life, most of their expectations were fulfilled.

disappointments: _____

Writing Activity

Write a brief summary of the life of this couple using adverb clauses of time. Use the comprehension questions in activity B to help you.

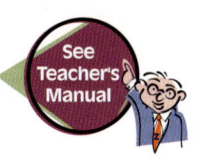

Lesson 7 — # FAMILY JOURNEYS

Pre-Reading Activity

PAIR WORK

Look at the pictures above and discuss the following questions with a partner. Take note of your answers. Then report to the class.

1. What are the people doing in the pictures above?
2. What are some of the differences between the two pictures?
3. Which of these forms of transportation seem more dangerous, more economical, and more practical? Explain.
4. What are the advantages and disadvantages of modern transportation?
5. Do you think modern transportation has had an impact on your travel to other countries?
6. What are the responsibilities of parents when traveling with their children?

7. How has traveling with a family changed in the past hundred years?

Journal Writing

A. Describe a journey that you took either with your family or alone that was very difficult. Write about it and refer to the questions:.

MY JOURNAL

√ Where were you going?
√ Who were you with?
√ When did this journey take place?
√ What was difficult about this journey?
√ How did you overcome this difficulty?
√ What did you learn about yourself from the experience?

B. PAIR WORK

Exchange journals with a partner. Read your partner's journal. Then write a response to your partner's journal in the space provided below. (Example: Think of the experience you had and describe how it was similar or different.).

PARTNER'S RESPONSE

Interactive Reading

A. GROUP WORK: Each student reads a different paragraph. The rest of the class listens, and comprehends the story and the meanings of the boldfaced words.

My Great-Grandparents and Their Journey

A. My great- grandparents, Peter and Gisela came to this country during the great European *migration* in the mid-to late 1800s. When they arrived in the United States, they realized that their lives were going to be very difficult but that there was the possibility to make their lives better through hard work and *determination*. Gisela, my great-grandmother was was from Germany, and she came here as a midwife accompanying a couple who were expecting their first child. Peter, my great- grandfather was from Ireland and came because of a *famine* that was *devastating* his country.

B. Peter's first job was as a street sweeper. He made three cents a day. It was a daily *struggle* to survive, and he would later *recount* the stories of his first days in this country to his children. Some nights he would go to sleep hungry on the steps of an apartment building next to his job. Many people were arriving in New York City, so *labor* was very cheap, and there were few jobs left for everyone else. The city was becoming crowded with newly arrived immigrants, and soon he was out of work and taking on *odd jobs*.

C. My great-grandparents met one day as he was sweeping the street and she was shopping for the child she was babysitting. After three years of living together in New York City, they got married. At first, they were **ambivalent** about their lives and surroundings, and decided to move out west because of the **deteriorating** conditions of the city. For the next seven years, they struggled to save enough money to buy a small **parcel** of land in Ohio. Together they packed all of their things in a wagon and made the long journey. They traveled with a large group of wagons for safety. After three weeks of **brutal** snow and difficult traveling conditions, they finally made it to the small track of land that they owned and began building their life together.

D. For the first couple of months, food was **scarce**. They had arrived in the middle of winter, and it took them two months to finally build a house that would keep them safe from the **elements**. They survived on the supplies they had brought with them on the long journey, but not long after, they were close to running out. Luckily, spring arrived before they had nothing left, so they were able to plant crops. Life became more **bearable**.

E. My great-grandparents had thirteen children. While their children would grow up and travel all over the United States and other parts of the world, my great-grandparents never moved again. My great-grandparents were part of the **pioneering spirit** that helped shape America and continues to draw people from all over the world. They came here with very little money, but with hard work and sacrifice were able to **carve out** a life for themselves and their family. They also provided valuable opportunities for their children and grandchildren.

Do you think the current immigrants in North America have experienced the same struggle?

B. PAIR WORK: Comprehension Questions

Work in pairs and answer the questions using the words in parentheses (adverb clauses of cause and effect).

1. Why did the author's great-grandparents come to the United States? (because)

   The author's great-grandfather came to the United States *because* there was a famine that was devastating his country, and his great-grandmother came *because* she was a midwife accompanying a couple who were expecting their first child.

2. Why did the author's great-grandfather lose his job? (since)

   _____
   _____

3. Why did the author's great-grandparents decide to move out of New York City? (since)

   _____
   _____

4. Why do you think the great-grandparents of the story traveled with a large group of wagons on their journey west? (because)

   _____
   _____

5. Why was the journey to the West so brutal? (because)

   _____
   _____

6. How did their lives become bearable? (since)

_____

_____

C. VOCABULARY IN CONTEXT

Read the sentences below and write the meanings of the boldfaced words based on the sentences provided. Then come up with sentences using the same vocabulary words.

1. Birds **migrate** from the north to the south every winter.
migrate: _____

_____

2. Our grandparents would **recount** the stories of their early lives in their native homeland.
recount: _____

_____

3. When you go to work, you become part of the **labor** force.
labor: _____

_____

4. He never has one steady job, but instead does a variety of non-permanent **odd jobs** like painting and carpentry.
odd jobs: _____

_____

5. Susan doesn't know how she feels about life in her new country. She is **ambivalent** about it.
ambivalent: _____

_____

6. The building is so old and its structure is **deteriorating**. It may collapse soon.

deteriorating: _____

_____

7. The winter in Wisconsin is **brutal**. It is cold and snowy all the time.

brutal: _____

_____

8. When food was **scarce** in the wintertime, pioneers suffered from hunger.

scarce: _____

_____

9. Pioneers had to build their own houses so they wouldn't be affected by the **elements**, such as wind, rain, snow, and hail.

elements: _____

_____

10. After a long winter, the first warm days make life **bearable** again.

bearable: _____

_____

11. My great-grandparents were part of the **pioneering spirit** that helped shape America and continues to draw people from all over.

pioneering spirit: _____

_____

12. By working hard, families on the frontier were able to **carve out** a life for themselves.

carve out: _____

_____

D. PAIR WORK: Discovering Main Ideas and Details

Match the following headings to the five paragraphs (A - E) of the previous essay. Then, write one detail which supports your choice of heading.

Heading	Paragraph (A – E)	Supporting Detail
Unknown future	C	The author's great-grandparents were ambivalent about their lives.
Almost disaster		
Tough life		
Spirit of America		
Why they came		

Writing Activity
PERSONAL STORY

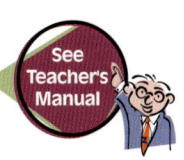

Write a three-paragraph short story about how you or your family's lives have changed since you have come here. Follow the format provided below. Use adverb clauses of cause and effect when possible. Write a topic sentence (main idea) for each paragraph.

> **Paragraph I : Daily life in the United States (now)**
>
> Describe your life in the United States. How do you spend your free time? Why do you choose to spend it that way?

Paragraph II: Life in your country (before)

Describe what your life was like before you came to the United States? Why did you take part in these activities?

Paragraph III: Differences or similarities between then and now

What is the difference between your life here and your life in your country? Explain.

Lesson 8: IMMIGRATION

Pre-Reading Activity

PAIR WORK
Discuss with your partner the following questions.

1. Do you know anyone who has emigrated to another country?

2. What are the steps for someone to immigrate to your country?

3. Are you interested in emigrating to another country? Explain.

Reading Exercise

A. GROUP WORK : Vocabulary in Context

Read with your group to find the definitions for the boldfaced words and put a one-word synonym in the box. Use contextual clues to understand the meaning of the words.

WILL IT ALL STAY THE SAME?

I remember the day when my family got off the plane in Vancouver, Canada, twenty years ago. It was my parents, my brother, and me. We had just traveled **halfway around the globe**[1] from Korea to start a new life. I was four years old. For the first half of my life, growing up in Vancouver, Canada, **as opposed to**[2] Pusan, Korea, did not seem so different. However, the normal **clash**[3] between parents and teenagers became **exaggerated**[4] because of the cultural differences between my parent's traditional expectations of a daughter and Canada's more **liberal**[5] social acceptance of young women.

A perfect example of this is something that happened when I was twenty-two years old. We visited Korea for the summer so my brother and I could spend time with our grandparents. My parents knew that I smoked. They didn't approve, but they had never expressed their **dissatisfaction**[6] with my choice to smoke. However, while in Korea, I stepped out of my grandmother's house and walked down the street to get some fresh air and smoke a cigarette. When I returned, my father was **furious**[7] and **scolded**[8] me for smoking in public. Apparently, in Korea it is still very much taboo for a woman to smoke out in the open.

Synonyms

1. _____
2. _____
3. _____
4. _____
5. _____
6. _____
7. _____
8. _____

After this incident, I could not wait to get back to Canada, where I felt freer and a lot less pressure from society. My brother, who was given a lot more freedom growing up than I was, has **adopted**[9] and **conformed**[10] to a lot of the standards my parents **imposed**[11] on us. Recently he got married and moved into our parents' home with his new wife. That seems to be the traditional thing to do for the eldest son in a Korean family.

9. _____
10. _____
11. _____

I have told my parents that next year I am going to begin a doctorate program for my PhD in child psychology. I know they are really proud of me and all that I have accomplished, but I still feel like they expected me to be married by now. Here in Canada, I do not feel the pressure that I do when I am in Korea. Recently my boyfriend and I have been talking about getting married. I am sure this will present challenges for me as well for my family, but I think we will be able to work through them.

B. GROUP WORK: Comprehension Questions

In groups of three, discuss the comprehension questions and share your group's answers in class.

1. Why was the normal clash between her and her parents exaggerated?

2. What is taboo for women to do in Korea?

3. How has her brother conformed to their parents' ideas?

4. What expectation did her parents have for her by now?

5. Do you think her boyfriend is Korean? Why or why not?

C. VOCABULARY EXERCISE
Use your dictionary to find the meaning of the following vocabulary words.

1. halfway around the globe
A very far distance to travel

2. as opposed to

3. clash

4. exaggerate

5. liberal

6. dissatisfaction

7. furious

8. scold

9. adopt

10. conform

11. impose

D. VOCABULARY EXPANSION

Read each sentence and fill in the correct vocabulary word. Use each vocabulary word just once. Change the part of speech if necessary. Then think of an appropriate **antonym** (opposite) for each word and write it next to the term.

as opposed to _____	clash _____
exaggerate _____	liberal _____
dissatisfaction _____	furious _____
scold _____	adopt _____
conform _____	impose _____

1. My friend is always __exaggerating__ his basketball stories. He said he scored sixty-five points yesterday, but really he only scored seven.

2. My brother was _____ when he found out I had borrowed his car without his permission. He hasn't spoken to me for three days.

3. The government recently _____ new limits on the number of immigrants that can enter the country.

4. The child was _____ by her mother for not looking both ways before crossing the street.

5. Some customs and activities are difficult to _____ to because they are so different from what I am used to in my country.

6. My best friend's boss thinks that he is lazy. He will have to _____ a new attitude at work if he wants to succeed.

7. Most people immigrate to a new country because they are

_____ with their current opportunities.

8. My friend does not have a good understanding about money. He gives

_____ to charities and barely has enough for himself.

9. My room is big and spacious _____ my brother's room, which is small and narrow.

10. My mother and younger brother _____ all the time about his future. He wants to play in a rock band, but she wants him to go to college.

E. WHAT WOULD YOU SAY?

Work with your partner. Read the situations. For each situation write what you would say using the vocabulary words. Fill in the blanks with the speakers and their conversation.

1. Your parents decide to immigrate to the United States.

(Person A): My parents are planning to immigrate *halfway around the globe*.

(Person B): Really? That's exciting. Are they going to *adopt* a new way of life?

(Person A): I guess they will try to *conform* to the new culture.

(Person B): As long as it does not *impose* on them, they should be okay.

2. You are hooked on smoking marijuana, and your parents want to disinherit you.

(   ): _____

(   ): _____

(   ): _____

(   ): _____

3. Your parents have made plans for your future, but you want to do something else.

(   ): _____

(   ): _____

(   ): _____

(   ): _____

4. You want to marry someone who has a criminal record. Your parents do not approve of him despite the fact that he is already a changed man.

(   ): _____

(   ): _____

(   ): _____

(   ): _____

5. You want to travel and visit other countries with the purpose of looking for a partner.

(   ): _____

(   ): _____

(   ): _____

(   ): _____

Writing Activity
Creating a Story

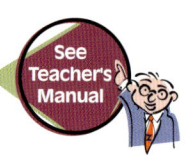

Pair Practice — See Teacher's Manual

PAIR WORK

Look at the pictures and then write a short story about each picture. What happened before the picture was taken? What will happen after? Be creative!

Read your short story aloud in class with the correct pronunciation and intonation.

Ex: I met my boyfriend in the park when we were both walking our dogs. It was love at first sight. Since then, we have been going back to the park every year on our anniversary. Next year we're going to get married in the same park, at the same spot where we met. We hope to have a very happy and fruitful life.

1.

2.

3.

4.

PAGE 78 LESSON 8 ZONI LANGUAGE CENTERS ©

Assessment

Family Values

Project — See Teacher's Manual

Research and write a story about a famous person who has had an impact on a country's history because of family values, traditions, beliefs, and practices. Find an interesting story about their family life and memorable experiences with their parents or siblings that greatly influenced their lives. Recount the story to your classmates.

What makes the heroes and heroines of American history famous and interesting are the fascinating stories, legends, and folktales that are told about them. For instance, George Washington is famous not only for being the first president but for never telling a lie. As the story goes, young George Washington chopped down a cherry tree on his father's plantation. When he was asked whether he had chopped down the tree, he did not try to deny it, but instead replied, "I cannot tell a lie, Pa. You know I cannot tell a lie. I did cut it with my hatchet." This story may or may not be true, but the important thing is that it shows the character of Washington as an honest child.

Grammar Review

Adverb Clauses of Time and Cause and Effect

TIME CLAUSES

When the phone rang, Maria was eating lunch.

By the time I got home last night, my family had already eaten.

Before we left for work in the morning, we had eaten breakfast.

Tony answered the letter **after his boss had told him it was important.**

CAUSE AND EFFECT

I started studying **because I wanted to learn English.**

Now that I have a new car, I can drive to the beach in the summertime.

Since Ming Jung's family is very conservative, she will get married only after completing university.

I was late **because it was raining.**

GLOSSARY

Vocabulary Word	Part of Speech	Pronunciation	Meaning
abandon	verb	[uh-**ban**-duh n]	to go away from without intent of returning
access	noun	[**ak**-ses]	the ability, right, or permission to approach, enter, speak with
adopt	verb	[uh-**dopt**]	to approve or accept a new idea from someone
ambivalence	adjective	[am-**biv**-uh-luh ns]	having mixed feelings about something
archetype	noun	[**ahr**-ki-tahyp]	original model from which others are copied
bearable	adjective	[**bair**-uh-buh l]	tolerable, endurable
brutal	adjective	[**broot**-l]	very cruel, merciless
carve out	phrasal verb	[kahrv] [out]	to make a great effort to accomplish something for the first time
civil engineer	noun	[**siv**-uh l] [en-juh-**neer**]	person who is skilled in the use of scientific knowledge for building roads, drainage systems, etc.
clash	verb	[klash]	conflict
concept	noun	[**kon**-sept]	idea
conform	verb	[kuh n-**fawrm**]	go along with the rules or general custom
conventional	adjective	[kuh n-**ven**-shuh-nl]	mainstream, traditional
deteriorating	adjective	[dih-**teer**-ee-uh-reyt]	falling apart; getting worse
determination	noun	[dih-tur-muh-**ney**-shuh n]	strong will to follow one's dreams
devastating	adjective	[**dev**-uh-stey-ting]	horrible; destructive
disappoint	verb	[dis-uh-**point**]	to fail to fill the expectations or wishes of
dissatisfaction	noun	[dis-sat-is-**fak**-shuh n huhn]	unhappy with the outcome of something
elements	noun	[**el**-uh-muh ns]	the weather, rain, wind, snow, etc.; natural environment and conditions
exaggerate	verb	[ig-**zaj**-uh-reyt]	making things seem larger or smaller than they really are; expanding on the truth
exchange	verb	[iks-**cheynj**]	to give one thing in place of another
extended family	noun	[ik-**sten**-did] [**fam**-lee]	family made up of members beyond parents and children; relatives such as grandparents, aunts, uncles, cousins
famine	noun	[**fam**-in]	extreme and general scarcity of food causing hunger and starvation
fortunate	adjective	[**fawr**-chuh-nit]	lucky
foundation	noun	[foun-**dey**-shuh n]	underlying principles or ideas on which something is based
function	noun	[**fuhngk**-shuh n]	purpose; how something works

furious	adjective	[fyoo r-ee-uh s]	very angry
halfway around the globe	idiom	[haf-wey] [uh-round] [the] [glowb]	a very far distance to travel
humanitarian work	noun	[hyoo-man-i-tair-ee-uh n] [work]	to work for the benefit of people
impose	verb	[im-pohz]	to force something to be accepted by others
labor	noun	[ley-ber]	work, people who work
liberal	adjective	[lib-er-uh l]	accepting of difference
love at first sight	idiom	[luhv] [at] [furst] [sahyt]	to feel like you are in love at the first moment you meet someone
migration	noun	[mahy-grey-shuh n]	moving from one area to another, usually in groups
mutual friend	idiom	[myoo-choo-uh l] [frend]	friend shared by two or more people
nuclear family	idiom	[noo-klee-er] [fam-lee]	center of the family made up of parents and children; immediate family
odd job	idiom	[od] [job]	non-permanent work
opposed to	adjective	[uh-pohz d too]	the opposite of
outward appearance	idiom	[out-werd] [uh-peer-uh ns]	what something looks like on the surface; surface of something
parcel	noun	[pahr-suh l]	a package, container, bundle, object
pioneering spirit	idiom	[pahy-uh-neer ing spir-it]	the feeling of early settlers in the United States that they could accomplish their goals and dreams by moving to the West
prime example	idiom	[prahyn] [ig-zam-puh l]	best example of something
raising children	idiom	[rey-zing] [chil-druh n]	bringing up children, teaching and caring for them
recount	verb	[ree-kount]	tell again
reunion	noun	[ree-yoon-yuh n]	uniting or coming together again
scold	verb	[skohld]	yell at, reprimand
struggle	noun	[struhg-uh l]	to fight against an opponent or a force
taboo	noun	[tuh-boo]	something that is forbidden within a given society
underlying	adjective	[uhn-der-lahy-ing]	fundamental, basic
universal	adjective	[yoo-nuh-vur-suh l]	something that is held as true in all societies
volunteer	verb	[vol-uh n-teerz]	to work for free, or freely help others

Source: Dictionary.com

UNIT 3

ALTERNATIVE MEDICINE

Health is Wealth

"Every human being is the author of his own health or disease."
—Hindu Prince Gautama Siddharta, the founder of Buddhism, 563-483 B.C.)

Info tip:
Chiropractic treatments were boycotted in the United States by the American Medical Association until 1987.

Lesson 9 — BEING HEALTHY

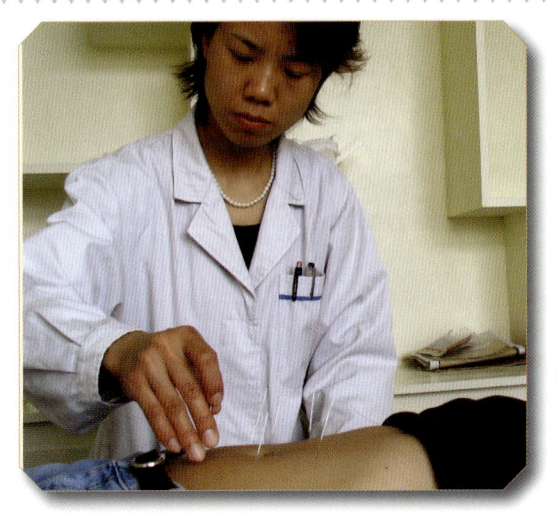

Pre-Reading Activity

GROUP WORK: Jigsaw
Work in groups. Discuss the following questions with your group and share your group's answers with the other groups in the class.

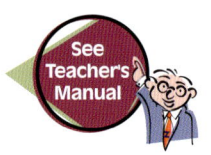

1. Look at the pictures above. What actions are being performed in these pictures?

2. Have you been treated by either of these types of medical practitioners?

3. What is more common in your country: Western medicine or alternative medicine?

4. What do you have more faith in: Western medicine or alternative medicine?

5. What is Western medicine good for? What is alternative medicine good for?

6. What are the different types of alternative medicine that are practiced in your country?

7. Have you heard about "faith healing?" What do you think about it? Do you think that people can be healed by faith healers? Are faith healers fake or real?

8. Do you know of any faith healers who can cure some ailments?

Journal Writing

A. Write about an experience you have had using a home remedy for any sort of sickness or ailment. Refer to the questions.

See Teacher's Manual

- √ What was the sickness?
- √ When did you have it?
- √ What did you use to cure it?
- √ Was it an easy or a difficult cure to use?
- √ Did it work?
- √ How long did it take?
- √ How do you feel about this remedy?

MY JOURNAL

B. PAIR WORK

Exchange journals with a partner. Read your partner's journal and write a response to what your partner has written. Is it similar in any way to what you have written? Have you heard of this remedy? Does it change your beliefs about using home remedies?

PARTNER'S RESPONSE

Reading Exercise

A. Read with your group to find the definitions for the boldfaced words and put a one-word synonym in the box. Use contextual clues to understand the meaning of the words.

Alternative Medicine

Alternative medicine is defined as medicine and medicinal practices that are based on historical, cultural, and **folklore**[1] as opposed to scientific evidence. There are many different kinds of **treatments**[2] that are considered alternative medicine. Some popular alternative medical treatments are acupuncture, homeopathy, and hypnosis. What all of these treatments have in common is that when they are tested under the same circumstances as Western medicine, they appear to have no more effect than a **placebo**[3]. They neither harm nor help the patient. Most practitioners and even patients of alternative medicine **dismiss**[4] those findings as the inability of Western methods to test the effectiveness of an alternative treatment. They argue the findings are limited and therefore can't be used to **gauge**[5] the effectiveness of alternative medicine. Some critics even go so far as to say that alternative medicines work only within the traditional group or culture that created it and therefore cannot be applied generally to everyone. However, as the popularity of alternative medicine grows, its acceptance within the Western medical community has also grown.

Much of what we know and understand of alternative medicine is based on hearsay and superstition. A lot of the negative portrayal of alternative medicine can be traced back to the 1800s when snake-oil salesmen would travel throughout North America selling potions that they claimed would cure anything but actually did nothing. This legacy has caused people to **assume**[6] that alternative medicine must be first viewed with **skepticism**[7]. Practitioners of modern medicine have done little to encourage the use of alternative medicine, and because of that, have kept the idea of alternative medicine from **gaining ground**[8]. In other nations and cultures, the learned master or guru would treat patients with herbs, massage, and other practices including cupping and acupuncture. These practitioners were accepted as sincere in their practices and were highly respected.

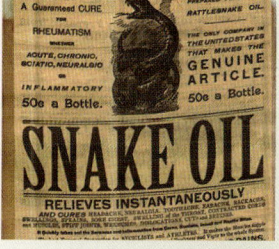

Notwithstanding, some alternative medicines have gained acceptance and are now considered part of the established Western medicine code. An example of this is chiropractic, which began as an alternative medicine but is now viewed as an established part of Western medicine. In fact, in the early 1970s the United States Congress **amended**[9] the Medicare Act to include chiropractic treatments so that they would be covered by Medicare and other private insurances.

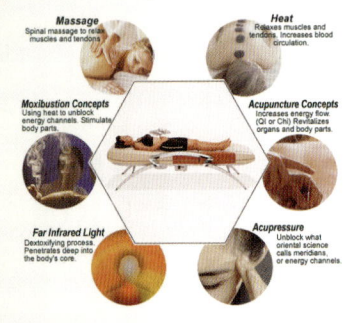

Alternative medicine continues to gain popularity, and in most surveys of people living in the United States and Canada, more than half of the **respondents**[10] reported trying some form of alternative medicine, and more than half said that they had had a positive experience and would use alternative medicine again.

Because of alternative medicine's growing popularity, scientists, governments, and businesses are constantly testing and evaluating the latest trends in alternative medicine in order to find cures and treaments for **ailments**[11] that have no Western medical treatment or cure. In most European countries, the government has tried to establish **guidelines**[12] and certification processes for practitioners of alternative medicine. This has gone a long way to challenge the view that alternative medicine should be viewed with **suspicion**[13]. In fact, because of the **spiraling**[14] cost of health insurance all over the world, governments are turning to more alternative medical solutions to supplement existing medical treatments. Laws have been passed in states like Texas and California that allow doctors to pursue alternative treatments that complement **prevailing**[15] standards. Doctors are beginning to feel greater freedom and less like **rogues**[16] when they prescribe acupuncture to treat some of the side effects of chemotherapy for cancer patients. The idea that practicing yoga and getting a massage can reduce stress and help treat insomnia is no longer frowned upon as idealistic but is being studied and seriously considered. If the current trend continues, then, what is considered alternative medicine today, will, in the future, be part of Western medicine.

As we learn more about the process of healing, we may find that there is more that can be discovered from the historical,

Synonyms

1. _____
2. _____
3. _____
4. _____
5. _____
6. _____
7. _____
8. _____
9. _____
10. _____
11. _____
12. _____
13. _____
14. _____
15. _____
16. _____

B. PAIR WORK: Comprehension Questions

<u>Scanning for details</u>: Scanning is looking at text for keywords to find specific information. Look at the comprehension questions below. Circle the key words in each question. Then scan the text for the matching words to answer the questions.

1. What are some types of alternative medicine practiced by many people?

_____

_____

2. Why do those who practice alternative medicine dismiss Western medicine's findings in regard to alternative practices?

_____

_____

3. What caused alternative medicine to be looked at negatively?

_____

4. What form of alternative medicine is now accepted as a legitimate form of medical treatment?

_____

5. What are governments and businesses constantly testing and evaluating?

_____

6. Which states have passed laws to allow doctors to use alternative treatments?

_____

7. What are some solutions to reduce stress and to help treat insomnia?

_____

Exchange your answers with other pairs in the class; then check as a group.

C. PREVIEWING THE TEXT: Skimming for Main Ideas

Skimming an article means reading the article quickly while trying to grasp the main ideas and major supporting details of the article. Read the article about alternative medicine and then write the main idea of the article on the line below. Then write two details which support the main idea.

See Teacher's Manual

MAIN IDEA

_____

_____

TWO SUPPORTING DETAILS OF THE MAIN IDEA

1. _____

2. _____

D. GROUP WORK: Sentence Construction

Work with your group to replace the boldfaced words with synonyms. Then use the words in sentences.

1. "Alternative medicine" is defined as medicine and medical practices that are based on historical, cultural, and **folkloric** traditions as opposed to scientific evidence.

   "Alternative medicine" is defined as medicine and medical practices that are based on historical, cultural, and *traditional stories* as opposed to scientific evidence.

2. There are many different kinds of **treatments** that are considered alternative medicine.

   _____

   _____

3. What all of these treatments have in common is that when they are tested under the same circumstances as Western medicine, they appear to have no more effect than a **placebo**.

   _____

   _____

4. Most practitioners and even patients of alternative medicine **dismiss** those findings as the inability of Western methods to test the effectiveness of an alternative treatment because they are limited, and therefore can't be used to **gauge** the effectiveness of alternative medicine.

   _____

   _____

5. Much of what we know and understand of alternative medicine is based on *hearsay* and superstition.

_____

_____

6. This legacy has caused people to *assume* that alternative medicines must be first viewed with *skepticism*.

_____

_____

7. Practitioners of modern medicine have done little to encourage the use of alternative medicine and, because of that, have kept the idea of alternative medicine from *gaining ground*.

_____

_____

8. In fact, in the early 1970s the United States Congress *amended* the Medicare Act to include chiropractic treatments under other private health insurance coverage.

_____

_____

9. Alternative medicine continues to gain popularity, and in most surveys of people living in the United States and Canada, more than half of the *respondents* reported trying some form of alternative medicine.

_____

_____

10. Because of alternative medicine's growing popularity, scientists, governments, and businesses are constantly testing and evaluating the latest trends in alternative medicine in order to find cures and treatments for *ailments* that have no Western medical treatment or cure.

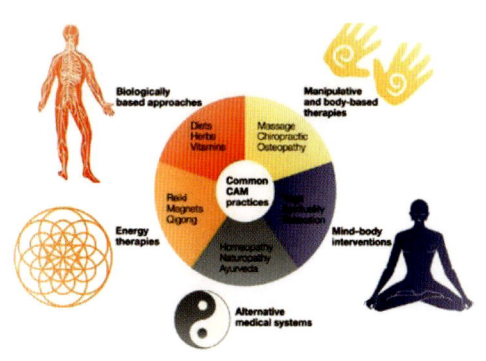

Image from www.nccam.nih.gov

_____

_____

_____

11. In most European countries, the government has tried to establish *guidelines* and certification processes for practitioners of alternative medicine.

_____

_____

12. This has gone a long way to challenge the view that alternative medicine should be viewed with *suspicion*.

_____

_____

13. In fact, because of the *spiraling* cost of health insurance all over the world, governments are turning to more alternative medical solutions to supplement existing medical treatments.

_____

_____

14. Laws have been passed in states like Texas and California that allow doctors to pursue alternative treatments that complement *prevailing* standards.

_____

_____

15. Doctors are beginning to feel greater freedom and less like *rogues* when they prescribe acupuncture to treat some of the side effects of chemotherapy for cancer patients.

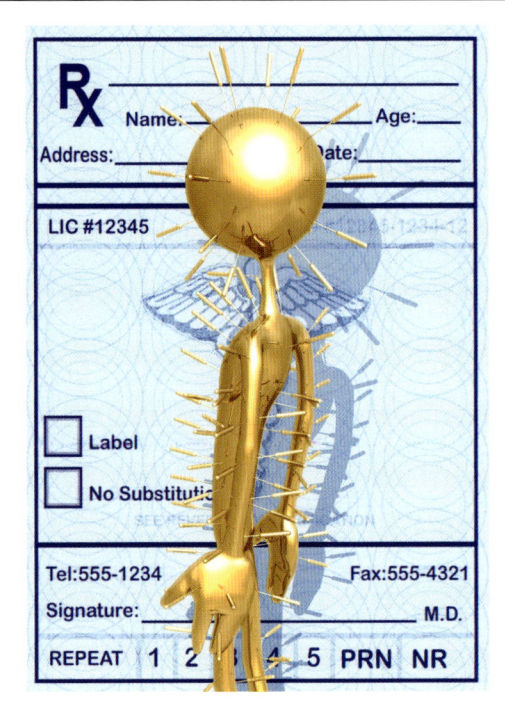

_____

_____

Writing Activity
Internet Research

Do research on the Internet on practitioners of alternative medicine or gurus who claim to have cured either physical or psychological illnesses. Choose two gurus, one sincere and one who seems insincere. Take notes on what you find. Then present your findings to the class. The class will vote to decide, based on your presentation, which practitioner is legitimate and which one is not. Include at least ten vocabulary words and their synonyms that were covered in this lesson.

Lesson 10 — Finding out the Facts

Pre-Reading Activity

GROUP WORK: Jigsaw
Work in groups. Discuss the following questions with your group and share your group's answers with the other groups in the class.

1. How do these people look in the pictures above? What adjectives would you use to describe them?

2. Do you consider yourself to be a healthy eater?

3. Have you ever taken an exercise class such as Yoga or Tai Chi?

4. Is a good mental attitude important for good health?

5. What is the most important part of anyone's lifestyle to have good health?

Journal Writing

A. Write about a person whom you go to when you want to discuss a problem or make a big decision. Refer to the questions.

MY JOURNAL

- ✓ Who is this person?
- ✓ How do you know him or her?
- ✓ What was the problem or decision you wanted to discuss?
- ✓ What advice did the person give you?
- ✓ How did the situation turn out?
- ✓ How did you feel after speaking to the person?

B. PAIR WORK

Exchange journals with a partner. Read your partner's journal and write a response to what your partner has written. Is it similar in any way to what you have written? Do you have a similar person whom you go to with problems or before you make any important decisions?

PARTNER'S RESPONSE

C. PAIR WORK: Information Gap Activity

What do you know about these various alternative therapies? Student A asks a question and student B answers. Student A writes the definition on the space provided. Reverse roles.

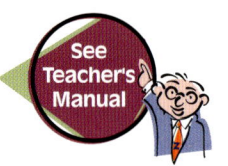

STUDENT A

Acupuncture

Question: What is acupuncture?

Answer:

This therapy is a traditional Chinese therapy that uses various techniques to clear the flow of Chi in the body.

This therapy is a Native American practice in which a small substance that copies the symptoms of an illness or disease is given to a patient. This is intended to stimulate the body's immune system to then fight off the disease.

Answer:

_____

_____

Herbalism

Question: What is herbalism?

Answer:

_____

_____

This therapy uses manipulation of the muscles and skeleton, particularly the spine, to improve general health.

Answer:

_____

_____

Aromatherapy

Question: What is aromatherapy?

Answer:

_____

_____

STUDENT B

This is a plant or plant mixture extract used to make medicine.

Answer:

_____

_____

Chiropractic medicine

Question: What is chiropractic medicine?

Answer:

_____

_____

This therapy uses plant oils, inhaled and applied, for physical and psychological health.

Answer:

_____

_____

Homeopathy

Question: What is homeopathy?

Answer:

_____

_____

This therapy is a traditional Chinese therapy that uses various techniques such as needling, cupping, and massage to clear the flow of Chi in the body.

Answer:

_____Acupuncture_____

_____

Zoni Times

Health — Issue 3, Vol 67

Reading Exercise

A. ROLE PLAY: Interview your partner using the dialogue. Then switch roles. Try to understand the interview and guess the meaning of the boldfaced words using contextual clues.

Acupuncture's Popularity on the Rise in the West

Acupuncture is one of the most popular alternative treatments used today. Based on the centuries-old traditional Chinese medicine and treatment, it can be used to **alleviate**[1] pain and **promote**[2] general wellness.

To find out more about acupuncture, and its **origins**[3], uses, and practices, we talked to Peter Caron, a student of acupuncture at a midtown Manhattan school of Chinese medicine.

Peter has been studying acupuncture for one year and has been a student of Chinese medicine for five years. He sat down to talk to us at a local coffee shop and shared his experiences and expertise on the topic.

Q: So, Peter, how did you become interested in Chinese medicine?

A: I like the philosophy that **underlies**[4] Chinese medicine a lot. I was a philosophy major in college and this was kind of a natural segue. Most of the people I know who do acupuncture seem very happy.

Q: How long does the training take?

A: The acupuncture training takes four years. At the end of the four years, there is a national exam that you have to take for **certification**[5].

Q: And once you are certified, are there different levels of acupuncturists?

A: Not really. Some states have particular requirements—for example, in California, you need to be able to **prescribe**[6] herbs, but in the rest of the country, you don't. But an

PAGE 102 — LESSON 10 — ZONI LANGUAGE CENTERS ©

acupuncturist is pretty much an acupuncturist. You can get a PhD in the field, but it doesn't change your scope of practice or your ability.

Q: So what things do you learn?

A: The school I chose has a pretty strong Western medicine focus, so about a third of it is about the same training a nurse would get—anatomy, physiology, pathophysiology, nutrition, and biochemistry at the level you would expect from a medical training institution. As far as the Chinese medicine goes, they have a different **concept**[7] that we have to learn. There are about six classes on acupuncture points. There are classes on **techniques**[8] for needling and for other Chinese medicine **modalities**[9] like cupping, and there are a lot of herb classes.

Q: Can you tell me about the history of acupuncture?

A: It's pretty heavily disputed. It goes back to an oral history. The earliest written record of acupuncture is arguably between 200 and 500 B.C. in the Huang Di Nei Jing, The Yellow Emperor's Classic of Chinese Medicine. And that's kind of the **foundation**[10] textbook for the philosophy that underlies Chinese medicine. Then after that it kind of gets into opinion about the history further. It looks as though it came from Indian medicine and changed heavily—the same way that Kung Fu came from Yoga, but there aren't really written records of that, so take that with a grain of salt. There have been a number of major evolutions in Chinese medicine since the Yellow Emperor's Classic. Most of them take the form of herb textbooks. There's the Treaties on Cold Damage, one of the first books that had to do with cities, and then there's Treatise on Heat Damage, which is, like, [about] really serious infectious diseases, and there's kind of an ongoing **evolution**[11] of Chinese medicine to where we are now.

Synonyms

1. _____
2. _____
3. _____
4. _____
5. _____
6. _____
7. _____
8. _____
9. _____
10. _____
11. _____

B. GROUP WORK: Reported Speech

Work with your group to answer the following comprehension questions. Change the quotes from Peter Caron to reported speech. Refer to the review of reported speech at the end of the unit. Use the question to begin your answer.

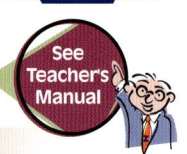

PART I: Writing answers for a question

Example:

A: Why did Peter Caron decide to study Chinese medicine and acupuncture?

B: Peter Caron decided to *study acupuncture because he liked the philosophy that underlay Chinese medicine a lot. He had been a philosophy major in college and this had been a natural segue. He also said that the people he knew who practiced acupuncture seemed very happy.*

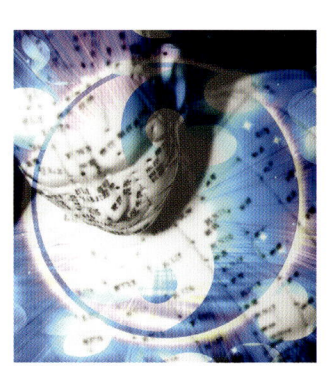

1. A: How long does the training take?

  B: Peter said that _____

2. A: Once you are certified, are there different levels of acupuncturists?

B: According to Peter, _____
_____
_____
_____

3. A: What things do acupuncturists learn?

B: Peter explained that _____
_____
_____
_____

4. A: What does Peter know about the history of acupuncture?

B: To Peter's knowledge, _____
_____
_____
_____

PART II: Writing Questions for an Interview

Read the rest of the interview written in reported speech. Based on the answers below, and using information questions—who, what, when, where, why, and how—guess what questions the reporter asked Peter Caron.

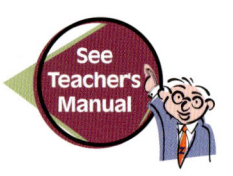

1. Question: When did acupuncture become an organized practice ?

Acupuncture didn't become an organized practice until the Communist Revolution in 1949. Before that, there were very *effective* but *specialized* schools and individual masters. However, after the revolution they sent people around to all of the counties in China and *compiled* [what they learned] into what is called Traditional Chinese Medicine (TCM).

2. Question: _____ ?

But actually, it's not really traditional Chinese medicine. It's more like modern Chinese medicine. The traditional Chinese medicine is called, Classical Chinese Medicine (CCM). The *contrast* is that this is more of a lineage or a family tradition. And there is often a lot more philosophical *depth* and more spiritual practices in the CCM teaching.

3. Question: _____?

There's this concept of Chi as an energy that moves through life. This energy also moves through you. When it is blocked, the result is disease. That's what Chinese medicine is about: getting people back to a free flow of Chi and to a lifestyle that never **hinders** the flow of Chi. And the idea is that if you **conserve** your Chi and protect it, you will have a very long and healthy life.

4. Question: _____?

Needles themselves don't do a lot at all. It's about how you **insert** them and where you insert them. The acupuncture points are about an inch below the skin. So you put the needle in, and you can actually feel the point when you get to it. It's almost like the needle jumps in your hand. And when you get to the point, you can actually see the needle stand up under the skin and start to **twitch** without [the patient] moving at all, which is really interesting.

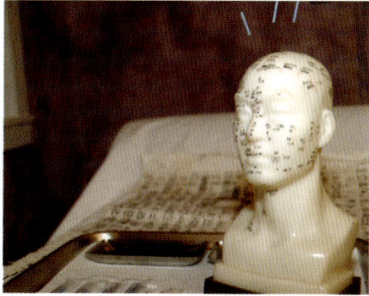

5. Question: _____?

We use massage. [And the other] main thing we use other than needling is cupping with glass cups. We heat the inside of the glass to create suction like a hot air balloon, put the cup on the skin, suck the skin into it, and then slide it around. If those things are there, you get bruising; if they are not there, you don't. So you continue this treatment in therapy until the person doesn't have any reaction at all, and at that point you've cleared the area. It generally takes three or four treatments.

6. Question: _____?

People were doing acupuncture here in the United States of America before, but they were doing it illegally. If you inserted those needles or owned those needles, the cops would show up and say, "What are you doing?" It wasn't till the late seventies that it really became something that people could do without a doctor's *supervision* or other *constraints*.

7. Question: _____?

There's both a serious dislike, an almost ***mocking*** attitude, toward acupuncture's apparent unscientific basis and a real feeling of being threatened by something that works that we don't really understand. [It] doesn't make sense in the Western perspective, and a lot of doctors see that and say this [acupuncture] is going against a lot of things they believe in really strongly. The ones that are open-minded enough say it doesn't matter what they think. It doesn't matter why it works, but for a lot of them, it's just really annoying.

8. Question: _____?

There's a lot of writing in the Chinese medical field about what Chinese medicine does that Western medicine doesn't, and vice versa. There are plenty of things I would go to the emergency room for, but Western medicine doesn't really have a concept of health. And Chinese medicine does well for those who are grossly ill, but it does better with those who are perfectly healthy. There's a passage in the Huang Di Nei Jing that says, "The greatest doctor appears to do nothing." If you can keep people from getting sick, that's really the ideal.

C. PAIR WORK: Scanning for Details

With a partner, scan the text for key words to find specific information. Look at the comprehension questions below. Circle the key words in each question. Then scan the text for the matching words to answer the questions. Compare and check your answers with your partner.

1. What is Chi?

_____

2. How do acupuncturists use needles?

_____

3. How does Peter explain Chinese diagnosis? (Choose one.)

      a. by giving a definition
      b. by giving an example
      c. by telling a story

4. How does the cupping technique work?

_____

5. How many cupping treatments are usually necessary?

_____

6. How would police react to finding people performing acupuncture before the 1970s?

_____

D. VOCABULARY EXPANSION

Complete the following summary of Peter Caron's interview using the words in the box below.

origins	certification	underlies
techniques	ridiculous	effectiveness
mock	foundation	alleviated
prescribing	complicated	specialists
techniques	supervision	promote

The philosophical 1) __foundation__ that 2) _____ the practice of acupuncture is Chinese medicine. Its purpose is to 3) _____ general health. It is most effective when used on people who are generally healthy.

Its 4) _____ date back to between 500 and 200 B.C. when master practitioners or 5) _____ used different 6) _____ to clear blockages in Chi. The symptoms were 7) _____ when the Chi was allowed to flow freely. Among the 8) _____ used are needling, cupping and 9) _____ herbs.

In modern times in the United States it was illegal to practice acupuncture without medical 10) _____. However, after the 1970s, it was accepted as a useful treatment. Now practitioners receive 11) _____ after taking a national exam.

Many practitioners of Western medicine believe acupuncture is 12) _____ and may even 13) _____ it, finding it annoying. However, it is a 14) _____ practice, and without study and practice, it is hard to have deeper understanding of its 15) _____.

E. EXPANSION ACTIVITY

Match the definitions in column B with the vocabulary words in column A.

COLUMN A		COLUMN B
1. compile	_g_	a. honestly
2. contrast	___	b. be involved in a deep and thoughtful way
3. depth	___	c. save
4. hinder	___	d. working well
5. conserve	___	e. pull with a light jerk; quiver or shake slightly
6. insert	___	f. prevent from happening
7. twitch	___	g. collect
8. frankly	___	h. put inside
9. efficacy	___	i. showing opposite of something

F. DIALOGUE PRACTICE

Work with your partner. Read the situations. For each situation, write what you would say using the vocabulary words.

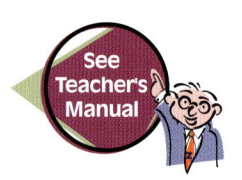

1. You are at the doctor's office.

   (Patient): Doctor, I still have a *twitch* in my arm.

   (Doctor): Have you felt the *efficacy* of the procedure?

   (Patient): *Frankly*, I haven't felt it yet. It's very difficult for me to follow your instructions.

   (Doctor): If you don't follow my instructions, it will *hinder* your progress.

2. You are explaining a new health product to your boss.

( ): _____

( ): _____

( ): _____

( ): _____

3. You are explaining to a class of students the benefits of an alternative medical treatment.

( ): _____

( ): _____

( ): _____

( ): _____

4. You are advising a friend not to try a new treatment.

( ): _____

( ): _____

( ): _____

( ): _____

5. You are preparing for a medical checkup.

( ): _____

( ): _____

( ): _____

( ): _____

Lesson 11: Interviewing an Expert

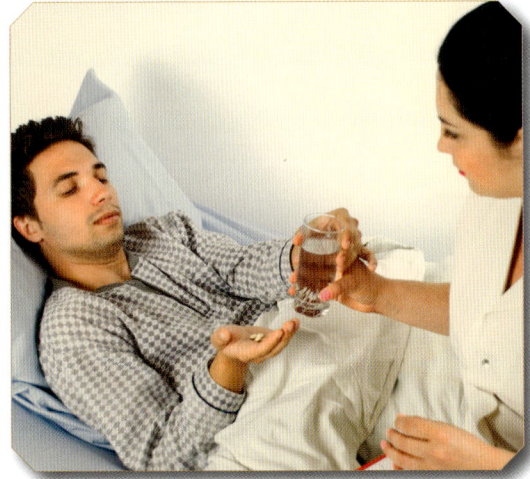

Pre-Reading Activity

GROUP WORK: Jigsaw
Work in groups. Discuss the following questions with your group and share your group's answers with the other groups in the class.

1. What are the most important qualities of a doctor?

2. Are you comfortable sharing personal information with your doctor to describe an illness?

3. What would you change about medical care in this country or in your home country?

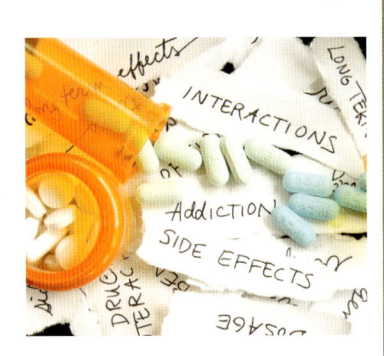

4. Do you worry that the medicine you are given by doctors has side effects?

5. Do you question your doctor's prescriptions for treatments and medicines?

6. What makes a person an authority figure: a title, a position in an organization, or public recognition?

Journal Writing

A. Write about an authority figure and refer to the questions.

√ Who is this person?

√ How do you know him or her?

√ Why do you view this person as an authority figure?

√ Do you look up to this person?

√ Why or why not?

MY JOURNAL

B. PAIR WORK

Exchange journals with a partner. Read your partner's journal and write a response to what your partner has written. Is it similar in any way to what you have written?

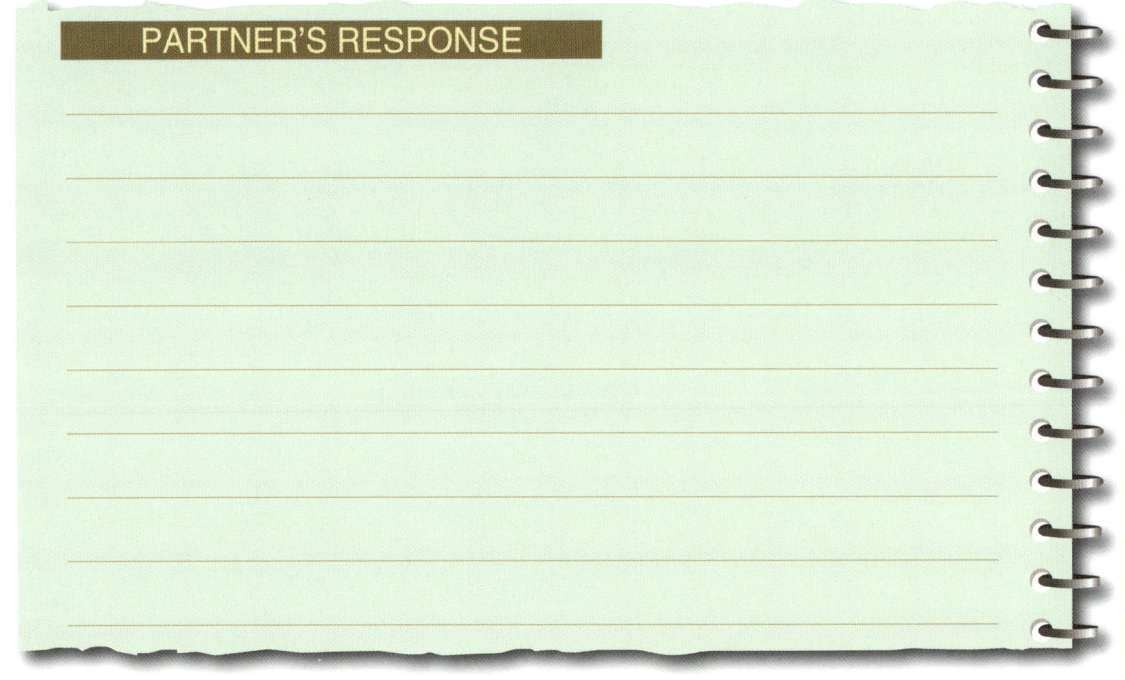

PARTNER'S RESPONSE

May 2010   **ZONI VOICE** ©

Health Interview

Interactive Reading

A. ROLE PLAY: Interview your partner using the dialogue. Then switch roles. Guess the meaning of the boldfaced words using contextual clues.

Group Work

See Teacher's Manual

A Doctor's Opinion on Alternative Medicine

Dr. Lestrino Cachola Baquiran agreed to meet with *Zoni News* and give his opinion on the various alternative medicine treatments available today. Dr. Baquiran has been a medical practitioner in New York City for the past forty years as an internist cardiologist.

Q: What do you think of alternative medicine?

A: I have no **objections**[1] to alternative treatments, especially not with acupuncture, because it's been there for thousands of years. It really does help some patients after Western medicine has failed them. I always have been surprised that patients really have been drawn to it, especially if they have **chronic**[2] pain, when different pain medications don't do the job. I think when they become particularly desperate, they try everything.

Q: Do your patients ask you about alternative medicine?

A: Yes. Alternative medicine is not **relatively**[3] recent but it's becoming more and more **prevalent**[4]. I think with the advance of the Internet, patients are becoming more informed, more **sophisticated**[5], and more educated about alternative medicine, so I think that that is the most important **trend**[6] in medicine. Of course, there have been horror stories about side effects of alternative medicine or even with medication that has been approved by the Food and Drug Administration (FDA). So [patients] come prepared sometimes, especially with vitamins, minerals, herbs. There is a new term now called **neutral chemicals**[7]. These are the ones that I find that patients begin the conversation with. The patients are the ones who **initiate**[8] the subject.

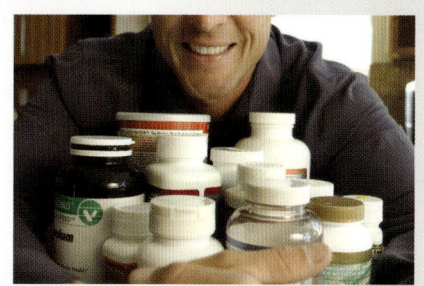

Q: Are you comfortable talking with your patients about alternative treatments?

A: Yeah. Why not? Most of these alternative medicines are not harmful, since the

ZONI LANGUAGE CENTERS ©   LESSON 11   PAGE 117

Health Interview

amounts are so little that they can only do good and very little **harm**[9]. My main concern is the lack of quality control, because they are considered food, not medicine, so there is a **spectrum**[10] of what you get, how much they're getting. You don't know. It's not **standardized**[11]. Different **practitioners**[12] have different preferences, different ways to administer the medicine, and different claims as to how effective they are.

Q: Have you heard of any problems associated with alternative treatments?

A: Some patients prefer to take non-prescription medicines or supplements to the point that they reject them for controlling blood pressure or cholesterol, or sometimes even for cancer prevention. But I tell them when they are really sick, the doses that they are getting are not effective and not **therapeutic**[13]. I think the best use for alternative medicine is for prevention.

The other thing is that some of these natural supplements contain substances that could **potentially**[14] be harmful. Some **stimulants**[15], sleep medications, even heart medication alternatives. I am always amazed the patients do not question if it's an herb, a vitamin, or a chemical. You give them a prescription and they object. They are worried about side effects. But I think the public should be aware that there are different levels of quality control. They are not really **regulated**[16] well enough.

Q: What should doctors know about alternative medicines?

A: The American Medical Association (AMA) has published a book. It's an **objective assessment**[17] about the effectiveness of alternative medicine. So you can see if claims have been confirmed. Many of these claims are not subject to the more expensive, more time-consuming, and more scientific trials that the FDA requires.

Q: Is there any treatment that you have reservations about?

A: As far as I'm concerned, the only one that I have a very negative aspect of is chiropractic, at least in my honest opinion. Patients seem to like it, accept it. If they don't have real problems in the spine, I usually discourage them from chiropractic until **nerve involvement**[18] has been ruled out.

Q: So if you were to rate alternative medicines from best to worst, where would you put these?

A: Acupuncture, being the oldest, is first. Next are herbalism and homeopathy, because the **doses**[19] are so low. If they're helpful, that's fine. Chiropractic, at the bottom.

Thank you, Dr. Baquiran!

B. PAIR WORK: Comprehension Questions

Work with a partner to answer the comprehension questions. Use complete sentences to answer the questions.

1. In general, how does Dr. Baquiran feel about alternative medicine?

   _____

   _____

2. How have patients' attitudes changed since the advances of the Internet?

   _____

   _____

3. According to Dr. Baquiran, who usually begins the conversation about alternative medicine?

   _____

   _____

4. What concerns does Dr. Baquiran have about the use of alternative medicine?

   _____

   _____

5. To what alternative treatment does Dr. Baquiran object the most? Why?

   _____

   _____

6. What are some problems that Dr. Baquiran sees with patients using alternative medicine?

_____

_____

7. How can doctors find out about the effectiveness of alternative medicines?

_____

_____

8. In his ranking of alternative treatments, which one does Dr. Baquiran put at the top of the list?

_____

_____

C. GROUP WORK: Vocabulary

Work with your group to write definitions of the words based on their context in the sentences.

1. The doctor raised no ***objections*** to using the alternative treatment, but just because he didn't say "no" to the treatment doesn't mean that he approved of it.

_____

2. He underwent acupuncture to alleviate his ***chronic*** back pain. After a few treatments, the constant pain that he had had for years went away.

_____

3. Homeopathy and herbalism are *relatively* safe. They may not help you, but they certainly can't hurt you. There are other treatments that are much more dangerous.

4. People today, especially since the beginning of the Internet, are so much more *sophisticated* than they were before. They know so much more about the world.

5. Medical trends are a lot like fashion *trends*: here today and gone tomorrow.

6. The first line of the Hippocratic oath is "First, do no *harm*." Doctors swear not to intentionally hurt any patient ever.

7. The *spectrum* of white light is the rainbow: yellow, orange, red, green, blue, indigo, and violet. That is, the colors that are contained in white light range from yellow to violet.

8. Today alternative medical practices outside of acupuncture are not *standardized*. There is no regular course of practice.

9. A medical *practitioner* knows about medicine and the patients he or she must treat.

10. While massage can feel good, does it really have any *therapeutic* benefits? Can it really heal your back?

_____

11. There are *potentially* thousands of solutions to that problem. We just have to find out which ones may work and which ones won't.

_____

12. The FDA strictly *regulates* medicine. There are countless rules and regulations controlling how medicine is used and if it is even allowed to be sold.

_____

13. We hope that doctors can make an *objective assessment* about alternative medicine and not allow their decision to be controlled by their own personal feelings.

_____

14. I was told to take three *doses* of the medicine, three times a day.

_____

15. Before the doctor could even ask the patient what was wrong, the patient *initiated* the conversation with questions about herbal remedies.

_____

D. GROUP WORK: Reported Speech

Work with your group to write a summary of the interview with Dr. Lestrino Baquiran using reported speech. Refer to the review of reported speech at the end of the unit.

Dr. Lestrino Baquiran said that he didn't have any objections to alternative treatments. He thought that it could help some patients.

E. GROUP DEBATE

Do you agree with Dr. Baquiran and his beliefs about alternative medicine? State your opinions on alternative medicine and share them with the class.

F. VOCABULARY EXPANSION

Read each sentence and fill in the correct vocabulary word. Use each vocabulary word just once.

objective	chronic	relatively
sophisticated	harmful	objective assessment
spectrum	standardized	practitioner
therapeutic	potentially	regulated
trend	doses	initiated

1. The current ___trend___ in medicine is for patients to do research before consulting a doctor.

2. _____ testing of medicine ensures that they will be tested the same way.

3. Some remedies may help patients, but others can _____ cause harm.

4. His _____ back pain has caused him to miss work on several occasions.

5. The Food and Drug Administration (FDA) has _____ the use and distribution of all prescribed medicine.

6. She _____ the discussion on alternative medicine at the insurance meeting.

7. There is a broad _____ of remedies for this particular illness.

8. Studying English has helped me to meet my _____ of becoming a doctor.

9. We live in a time when people are more _____ and worldly because of our access to information through technology.

10. Some exercises can yield beneficial, _____ results.

11. The _____ of homeopathic medicine that the patient received were not enough to cure her.

12. A good medical _____ knows about the body, disease, and how to talk to patients.

13. Medicine today is _____ less expensive than it was ten years ago.

14. Taking several different drugs can be potentially _____.

15. Scientists are required to make an _____ of medical treatments despite their personal feelings.

G. DIALOGUE PRACTICE

Work with your partner(s). Read the situations. For each situation, write what you would say using the vocabulary words.

1. You don't want to continue using a certain treatment prescribed by a doctor.

(Patient): Doctor, I'm worried about the *dosage* I'm receiving for this new drug. It seems too strong for me.

(Doctor): Well, that dosage meets the standard prescriptions for your height and weight.

(Patient): I understand, but I've read that it could *potentially* have harmful side effects.

(Doctor): Well, there is a broad *spectrum* of other drugs we could try if it would make you feel better.

2. You want your doctor to recommend another treatment for a condition.

(   ): _____

(   ): _____

(   ): _____

(   ): _____

3. You have taken some vitamins, and after a week, you have felt some side effects.

(   ): _____

(   ): _____

(   ): _____

(   ): _____

4. You have just started a new exercise routine and would like to recommend it to a friend.

(   ): _____

(   ): _____

(   ): _____

(   ): _____

Writing Assignment
Interviewing an Expert

Using the practices from the previous and current lesson on writing questions and reported speech, interview your classmate about something that he or she is an "expert" on. Write seven questions for the person to answer. Write down his or her responses carefully, and then write up a short interview in which you report his or her answers. Share with the class.

Reading Activity

A. PAIR WORK

Read the story with your partner. Have you had any similar experiences or do you know of a friend or a relative who was in a similar situation? Share your story with your partner.

ER
(Emergency Room)

I was recently in a car accident, and while the experience was difficult, the experience in the hospital was a lot more traumatic and scary. My friend and I were returning from a baseball game. We were driving down the highway when we swerved off the road. We were both alive, so we were very lucky, but my arm was in pain and my friend was having trouble standing. A car that passed us called 911, and soon there were two ambulances.

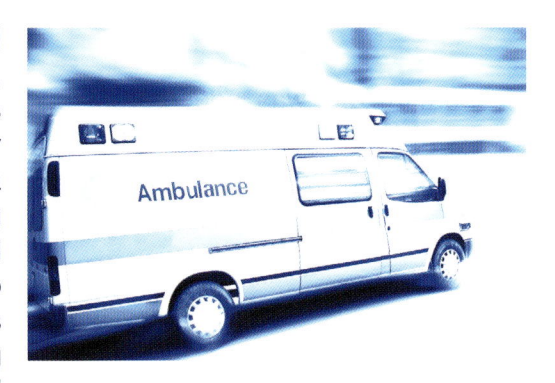

They took us to the emergency room. In the emergency room, we filled out some paperwork, and the nurse said that she would attend to us right away; instead, we waited. In fact, it had been three hours before we saw the nurse again. She told us that the emergency room was very crowded now and that we would have to wait because our injuries were not life threatening. I tried to move my arm and found that even after three hours, I was still in considerable pain.

When I finally saw a doctor, he asked me three questions: what happened, how I felt, and if I was allergic to any medication. I answered that I had been in a car accident, that my arm hurt, and that I was not allergic to any medication. He nodded, smiled, and said he would be back. Two hours later, he returned with a prescription and did a few more checks to see if any other parts of my body hurt. By this time, I had been in the hospital all night. I was tired, grouchy, and in pain. The doctor gave me some painkillers and signed a few papers before telling me that I needed to have an X-ray done to be sure that nothing was wrong. He left, and I waited for another hour before the X-ray technician came and took me where he was going to administer the X-ray. It took about thirty minutes, and the technician told me that he would be right back with the results. But this time I knew better! And just like I thought, he returned after two hours with the doctor. The doctor said that my arm was indeed broken and that I would have to wear a cast for three months. My friend was never admitted because he was just treated for a minor foot sprain.

The doctor spoke as he made the cast, and soon I found myself at the front desk of the hospital checking myself out. I had spent the entire night in a hospital just for a broken arm. I didn't have insurance, so I was a little worried about how much it would cost. My initial guess was that it would be anywhere from $300 to $500. One week later I got the bill: $5,400! I was in shock. How was I going to pay for this, and why was it so expensive? I couldn't believe it! What was I going to do?

B. GROUP WORK: Discussion Questions

Work in groups. Discuss the following questions with your group and share your group's answers with the class.

1. Have you ever been to a hospital in the United States or in your country? Describe your experience.

2. Do you have medical insurance? How does it work in your country?

Writing Assignment
Personal Experience

Have you or someone you know had a similar experience about going to a hospital for an emergency treatment in the United States or in your country? Write about it referring to questions such as what was the ailment, what was the treatment, how was the overall experience, how much was the bill, and so on.

Share your story with your partner.

Assessment

Famous Inventors

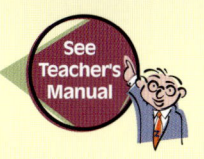

Inventiveness and ingenuity have always been an important part of American culture. This inventiveness is important not only in business and trade, but also in the areas of medicine and treatment. The American History Project will now focus on famous doctors and scientists in American history and their most famous medical practices and inventions. For this part of the project, do Internet research on a famous American doctor and his or her famous discovery, practice, treatment, or invention. Explain who the person is, give a description of him or her, tell an interesting story about his or her life, and explain the impact of his or her scientific discoveries.

For instance, a famous African American scientist/botanist is George Washington Carver (January 1864—January 5, 1943), whose most famous work was done on cultivating peanuts in the southern part of the United States. He was a fascinating person not only because of his discoveries but also because he was African American, born just as slavery was ending in the South.

Grammar Review

Quoted (Direct) Speech and Reported (Indirect) Speech

Changing quoted speech to reported speech.

RULE:

- When changing quoted speech to reported speech, the verb tense goes one step back. In other words, present tense verbs become past tense, past tense verbs become past perfect. When reported sentences express a general truth, the present tense is used in the main verb.

Examples:

- Dr. Baquiran said, "I have no objections to alternative treatments."

    Reported: Dr. Baquiran said that he had no objections to alternative treatments.

- Peter Caron said, "Acupuncture training is four years. My previous training was in Chinese massage and Tai Chi.

    Reported: Peter Carton explained that acupuncture training is four years and that his training had been in Chinese massage and Tai Chi.

GLOSSARY

Source: Dictionary.com

VOCABULARY WORD	PART OF SPEECH	PRONUNCIATION	MEANING
ailment	noun	[**eyl**-m*uh* nt]	physical disorder or illness
alleviate	verb	[*uh*-**lee**-vee-eyt]	make easier to endure, lessen
amend	verb	[*uh*-**mend**]	alter, change, modify, improve
aside	adverb	[*uh*-**sahyd**]	in spite of, apart from, notwithstanding
assessment	noun	[*uh*-**ses**-m*uh*nt]	evaluation
assume	verb	[*uh*-**soom**]	to take for granted without proof
certification	noun	[ser-tif-*uh*-**key**-sh*uh*n]	an official document that says someone is allowed to do a job
chronic	adjective	[**kron**-ik]	constant; habitual
compile	verb	[k*uh*m-**plahyd**]	to group together in a logical order
complicated	adjective	[**koom**-pli-kay-tid]	difficult to analyze, understand, or explain
conserve	verb	[k*uh*n-**surv**]	not waste; save, limit the use of
contrast	verb	[k*uh*n-**trast**]	to compare in order to show difference
deficient	adjective	[dih-**fish**-*uh*nt]	not enough of something; lacking; inadequate
depth	noun	[**depth**]	complexity, seriousness, gravity; having substance or thoughtfulness
diagnosis	noun	[dahy-*uh*g-**noh**-sis]	the decision that a doctor makes after examination, as to the kind or type of disease
dose	noun	[**dohs**]	the quantity of medicine prescribed to be taken
effective	adjective	[ih-**fek**-tiv]	producing an expected result
efficacy	noun	[**ef**-i-kuh-see]	capable of producing a desired result
evolution	noun	[ev-*uh*-**loo**-sh*uh*n]	growth, development and change over time
folklore	noun	[**fohkb**-lohr]	the traditional beliefs, legends customs of a group of people
foundation	noun	[foun-**dey**-sh*uh*n]	the basis of anything
frankly	adverb	[**frangk**-lee]	openly, honestly, plainly
gaining ground	idiom	[**geyn**-ing] [**ground**]	becoming more popular
gauge	noun, verb	[**geyj**]	figure out the strength, size, capacity, quantity etc. of something; estimate
guideline	noun	[**gahyd**-lahyn]	any rule that explains how something should happen
harm	verb	[**hahrm**]	cause physical injury or mental damage
hearsay	noun	[**heer**-sey]	unproven, unofficial information; gossip
hinder	verb	[**hinb**-der]	to cause delay, interruption or difficulty; to prevent from doing
initiate	verb	[ih-**nish**-ee-eyt]	to begin, set going, start, or originate
insert	verb	[in-**surt**]	to put or place into something

Word	Part of Speech	Pronunciation	Definition
mock	verb	[mok]	make fun of
modality	noun	[moh-**dal**-i-tee]	type of a treatment, usually physical therapy
objection	noun	[uhb-**jek**-shuhn]	reason or argument offered in disagreement, opposition
objective	adjective	[uhb-**jek**-tiv]	not influenced by personal feelings
origin	noun	[**awr**-i-jin]	the source or beginning of something
potentially	adverb	[puh-**ten**-shuh-lee]	possibly but not yet actually achieved
practitioner	noun	[prak-**tish**-uh-ner]	person who is practicing a profession like a medical practitioner
prescribe	verb	[pri-**skrahyb**]	to write down a rule or a course of action to be followed, especially medical
prevailing	adjective	[pri-**vey**-ling]	current, or having superior power or influence
promote	verb	[pruh-**moht**]	to encourage to exist or flourish
regulate	verb	[**reg**-yuh-leyt]	control with a rule, principle, or method
relatively	adverb	[**rel**-uh-tiv-lee]	as compared to something similar
respondent	noun	[ri-**spon**-duhnt]	person who answers questions as for a survey
ridiculous	adjective	[ri-**dik**-yuh-luhs]	absurd, laughable
rogue	noun	[rohg]	dishonest person, scoundrel, disobedient
route	noun	[root]	way, road, passage, path; life path
skepticism	noun	[**skep**-tuh-siz-uhm]	having doubt about something
sophisticated	adjective	[suh-**fis**-ti-key-tid]	having ideas, manners, education, worldliness
specialist	noun	[**spesh**-uh-list]	person who devotes himself or herself to one subject or particular area of study
spectrum	noun	[**spec**-truhm]	a broad range of varied but related ideas
spiraling	adjective	[**spahy**-ruhl]	advancing or increasing quickly; steadily rising
spirituality	noun	[spir-i-choo-**al**-i-tee]	feeling of connection or dedication to God, religion, spiritual values
standardized	adjective	[**stan**-der-dahyz]	following a rule which makes all things of a certain kind the same as each other
supervision	noun	[soo-per-**vizh**-uhn]	overseeing, organizing, managing of tasks or people
suspicion	noun	[suh-**spish**-uhn]	feeling that someone is probably guilty of a crime; feeling that something is probably wrong
technique	noun	[tek-**neek**]	special skill or way of doing something
therapeutic	adjective	[ther-uh-**pyoo**-tik]	having the ability to treat or cure a disease
treatment	noun	[**treet**-muhnt]	applying medicines, surgery, or other therapies to cure or manage a disease
trend	noun	[trend]	fashion, style, the general way that something is going
twitch	verb	[twitch]	pull with a quick short movement

UNIT 4

In Pursuit of Happiness

"Happiness never decreases by being shared."
—Buddha

Info tip:
According to Forbes.com, the ten happiest countries are also some of the wealthiest. How do these findings relate to your country?

1. Finland	Europe
2. Norway	Europe
3. Denmark	Europe
4. Iceland	Europe
5. Switzerland	Europe
6. Netherlands	Europe
7. Canada	Americas
8. New Zealand	Asia
9. Sweden	Europe
10. Australia	Asia

Lesson 12 — WHAT IS HAPPINESS?

Pre-Reading Activity

GROUP WORK: Jigsaw
Work in groups. Discuss the following questions with your group and share your group's answers with the other groups in the class.

1. What do you think of the pictures?

2. Are you happy? What is something that makes you happy?

3. Who is someone famous that you think is happy? Why?

4. Is being happy important in your life? How will you achieve it?

5. Can someone else make you happy? How?

6. What do you think is the color of happiness? Why?

Journal Writing

A. Write about one of the happiest events in your life. Refer to the questions.

- √ What was it that really made you very happy?
- √ Why did you feel very happy? Describe your feelings using colors and shapes.
- √ In what ways can you give or bring happiness to someone?
- √ Rank according to priority the factors that make you happy (e.g. love, money, family, children, friends, church, job and so on.)

MY JOURNAL

B. PAIR WORK

Exchange journals with a partner. Read your partner's journal and write a response to what your partner has written. Is it similar in any way to what you have written? Do you know of a similar person who has had the same experiences of happiness as you have?

PARTNER'S RESPONSE

Interactive Reading

A. GROUP WORK: Each student reads a different paragraph. The rest of the class listens, and comprehends the story and the meanings of the boldfaced words.

The Pursuit of Happiness

Happiness is **characterized** as the feeling of positive satisfaction, love, and **contentment**. If you ask one hundred people what it is that makes them happy, you will get one hundred different answers, and each answer is correct. Happiness is a **subjective** concept that has different meanings for different people. What makes people happy and how happiness is achieved have been the subject of debate and **fascination** for people throughout all of human history. Philosophers and scientists have tried to *quantify* and *qualify* happiness *to no avail*. Religious leaders and politicians have used the idea of happiness to *amass* followers. In fact, the United States of America was founded by people who were *persecuted* for their religious and political beliefs so that they could practice their beliefs and *pursue* happiness. "Americans' pursuit of happiness can be *broken down* into five common goals." Family, economics, personal goals, social interactions, and spirituality are the primary five *criteria* that most Americans believe will make them happy.

Most people believe that their happiness comes from their family. This is true not only for Americans but for most people, no matter what country or culture they come from. The family is a source of happiness for many reasons, but mainly it is looked at as a source of *companionship*, loyalty, and stability. Family members provide support for other members in the family, and this is why most people feel that if they have a strong and loving family, they have a greater opportunity to find happiness. This pursuit of happiness is perceived as a motivating reason to create a family of ones own. However, this goal of familial happiness can also be the *catalyst* for a large amount of pain, heartache, and personal problems. In fact, most people also choose family as the main reason for their sadness or melancholy. Therefore, while family is a reason to be happy, we also see it as a means of great amounts of stress and problems. This paradox is typical because it is usually present whenever there is a large personal investment such as there is within a family.

Your economic status can also be the source of happiness. Many people think personal happiness is *synonymous* with the success of their financial *endeavors*, and most people believe that they would be happier if they had more money. It is difficult to make assumptions about happiness if you have never had a ***relative*** experience. Studies on happiness and money have shown that there is no greater range of happiness for people who have money as opposed to those who don't, but money and wealth continue to be a ***perceived*** measurement of happiness for many people. In most Western developed countries, there is a greater rate of depression and suicide than in less wealthy countries. This can be seen as a possible ***de facto*** argument that money does not equal happiness. In truth, the ***catalyst*** for happiness is most likely stability and an ability to provide for those you care about. In this regard, your ability to financially support yourself and your loved ones could have a direct effect on your happiness.

Our personal lives are also an important factor of our happiness. It is through our personal development and our relationships that we find happiness. This was stated as one aspect of Maslow's ***hierarchy*** of needs. The fulfillment of our personal goals causes us to be content, and in turn creates happiness that we share with others. In situations where people are unable to fulfill their dreams and pursue their goals, they are more likely to be ***plagued*** by unhappiness than those who can follow their dreams and have opportunities to achieve them. Even through struggle and difficulties, if people believe that they have an opportunity to achieve their goals, they characterize their lives as happy. This is important because it means that if ***bereft*** of goals and opportunity, people are more likely to be unhappy.

Happiness is also created through interactions and social relationships. Sometimes the relationship is just two friends talking and sharing their life experiences with each other. Other times social relationships are created out of needs like helping someone less ***fortunate*** than you, or helping a child or an elderly person. Great satisfaction can come from helping others, and that, in turn, can lead to happiness.

Many times we feel that happiness is a selfish goal, but when we have the opportunity to help others become happy and live better lives, we can be happy as well.

Religion is also a place that many people turn to in order to find happiness. Religion gives us happiness by presenting meaning for our existence and focusing people on what is expected or required of them to live happy lives. When we examine these five essential spheres *of* happiness, we can see that it is very difficult to make assumptions about the lives and happiness of others. While a rich person may be unhappy because of a bad family relationship, a poor person could have very strong social relationships and be content. All of these criteria are connected to each other and can only be used subjectively to measure happiness. In reality, your own happiness can only truly be measured by you.

B. PAIR WORK: Comprehension Questions

Answer the questions with complete sentences and discuss with your partner.

1. What is happiness?

2. What are the top five factors that make people happy?

3. Which one of the five factors makes you the happiest?

4. Why do people choose family as a way to make them happy?

5. What is the difference between personal happiness and social happiness?

6. Can someone be happy with no money? Can a homeless person be happy?

7. Can an undocumented person be happy?

8. In general, are Americans and Canadians happy?

C. VOCABULARY IN CONTEXT

Write the meaning of the words according to how they were used in context.

1. John **characterized** his relationship with his girlfriend as loving, with a lot of give-and-take.

   characterized: _____

2. Elizabeth felt **contentment** with the arrival of a gift from her boyfriend, who is traveling and studying English in the United States.

   contentment: _____

3. Happiness is a **subjective** concept that has different meanings for different people.

   subjective: _____

4. It is hard for Mary to hide her **fascination** with the new city in which she lives now.

   fascination: _____

5. Scientists can't measure happiness because it is impossible to **quantify**.

   Quantify: _____

6. When I decided to attend college, I discovered that I **qualified** for a scholarship and a few grants.

   Qualified: _____

7. I tried to prove that happiness doesn't exist, but it was **to no avail**.

   to no avail: _____

8. John believed that in order to be happy he had to **amass** as much money as he could before he died.

amass: _____

9. Great men and women who try to change the world with their unusual ideas are usually **persecuted** because of their beliefs.

persecuted: _____

10. Before I began to **pursue** a music career, I studied the trends of the industry.

pursue: _____

11. Americans' pursuit of happiness can be **broken down** into five common goals: family, economics, personal goals, social interactions, and spirituality.

breaks down: _____

12. When you look for a job, you must be aware of the **criteria** that the employer is looking for on your résumé.

criteria: _____

13. The family is a source of happiness for many reasons, but mainly it is looked at as a source of **companionship** and stability.

companionship: _____

14. Wanting to live on his own, without a roommate, was the **catalyst** for John to find a new job.

catalyst: _____

15. Many people relate personal happiness to their financial **endeavors**.

endeavors: _____

16. It is difficult to make assumptions about happiness if you have never had a *relative* experience.

relative: _____

17. Manuel arrived at the concert late and *perceived* that the band hadn't begun to play yet because everyone was still waiting around the stage.

perceived: _____

18. Emily is the only woman at the party, so by *de facto*, she could be the only one in the woman's bathroom.

de facto: _____

19. As a new employee, Brandon had a difficult time understanding the company *hierarchy*.

hierarchy: _____

20. John has been *plagued* with a bad back ever since he played football in college.

plagued: _____

21. When people are *bereft* of the ability to pursue their goals and dreams, it is difficult for them to find happiness.

bereft: _____

22. I am very *fortunate* to have a lot of friends and family that love and care about me.

fortunate: _____

D. PAIR WORK

With a partner write a paragraph about the topic sentence using at least three of the vocabulary words in the box.

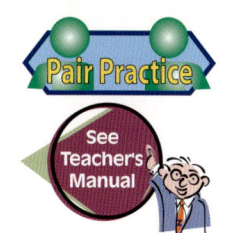

1. Money makes me happy.

characterized bereft perceived companionship subjective criteria	People have always *perceived* that money is bad, but it never leaves me *bereft* of *companionship*. What makes people happy is very *subjective*.

2. Having a supportive and loving family is what makes me happy.

fortunate hierarchy de facto break down relative contentment	

3. Achieving my personal goals makes me happy.

plagued endeavors catalyst amass pursue avail	

4. Having friends whom I can trust makes me happy.

quantify companionship to no avail fascination persecuted qualified	

ZONI LANGUAGE CENTERS © LESSON 12 PAGE 145

E. WHAT WOULD YOU SAY?

Work with your partner. Read the situations. For each situation, write a dialogue with your partner.

1. Your best friend is a successful banker on Wall Street, but he committed fraud. What would you say?

   (Michael): You look stressed out, relative to how you looked last month.

   (Joan): I'm *plagued* with a serious problem!

   (Michael): You are *fortunate* to have a job in this bad economy.

   (Joan): Not anymore. I have to face this problem or I can no longer *pursue* my goal.

2. Your best friend is alone for the holidays. What would you say?

   (   ): _____

   (   ): _____

   (   ): _____

   (   ): _____

3. Your friend's mother, who lives in Spain, passed away and you can't go to the funeral because of your visa status. What would you say to her?

   (   ): _____

   (   ): _____

   (   ): _____

(   ): _____

4. You have been working very hard at your job, but your weekly hours have been reduced. What would you say? How would you express your negative feelings?

(   ): _____

(   ): _____

(   ): _____

(   ): _____

5. Your boyfriend or girlfriend wants to get married, but you are not ready yet. What would you say?

(   ): _____

(   ): _____

(   ): _____

(   ): _____

6. Your classmate's sister, who has a great family and who is wealthy, has been diagnosed with depression. What would you say?

(   ): _____

(   ): _____

(   ): _____

(   ): _____

Lesson 13 — WHAT MAKES YOU HAPPY?

Pre-Reading Activity

GROUP WORK: Jigsaw

Work in groups. Discuss the following questions with your group and share your group's answers with the other groups in the class.

1. Where do you like to go to be happy? Why?

2. Who is someone in your family who always makes you happy?

3. Do you have friends in the United States who really make you happy?

4. Could you be happy living in another country forever? How?

5. What would make you the happiest person on earth?

Journal Writing

A. Write about a few big changes in your life and how you were able to adjust. Refer to previous experiences such as growing up, living independently, going to college, leaving your family or friends, getting married, ending a relationship, and so on.

MY JOURNAL

B. PAIR WORK

Exchange journals with a partner. Read your partner's journal and write a response to what your partner has written. Is it similar in any way to what you have written?

PARTNER'S RESPONSE

_____
_____
_____
_____
_____

Interactive Reading

A. Each student reads a different paragraph. The rest of the class listens, and comprehends the story and the meanings of the boldfaced words.

The Triumphant Story of Carmen

The life of Carmen Ruiz is a modern American success story. She was born in Cuba and immigrated to Miami when she was eight years old with her father, mother, and three *affable* brothers. In Cuba her family was *affluent,* but times were very difficult for them when they first arrived in the United States. Carmen's father and older brother looked for work but were unsuccessful, mainly because they didn't speak English very well, and soon the family was **afflicted** with poverty. After an **arduous** three months, Carmen's mother was able to find work as a nanny, and slowly the family began to become accustomed to their new life in America.

In Cuba, Carmen loved to watch her mother and father dance. Her father would be sitting watching television and her mother would dance in front of him, blocking his view. Her father would **pretend** that this **agitated** him, but it really didn't. Secretly, Carmen thought her father loved to watch her mother dance also. **After a spell**, her father would **acquiesce,** and they would dance salsa in the kitchen while Carmen and her brothers **giggled** and laughed at them. It's because of these **fond** memories that Carmen decided to become a professional dancer. Her family, however, didn't have enough money to send her to dance school. Carmen set aside her dreams of being a professional dancer and enrolled at the local community college where she studied **diligently** and became a nurse.

One day a patient who had been involved in a car accident came into the hospital where Carmen was working. He was unconscious. She tried to move him to a bed in the emergency room but his body was heavy, limp, and **aqueous**. She fell to the ground still holding him in her arms. He woke up at that moment, they looked into each other's eyes, and in an instant Carmen knew that she was in love. It **turns out** that the patient was named Tony Romero, and over the next two weeks, Carmen and Tony would spend a lot of time together as he recovered from his surgeries. When Tony was finally released, he **proposed** to Carmen. One month later they got married, and Carmen and Tony danced together for the rest of their lives.

B. PAIR WORK: Comprehension Questions
Answer the questions with complete sentences and discuss with your partner.

1. Where was Carmen Ruiz from?

2. Why couldn't Carmen's father find work?

3. What job did Carmen's mother have?

4. What did Carmen's parents do to have fun?

5. How did Carmen and Tony meet?

6. Is Carmen happy? Why?

C. VOCABULARY BUILDING
Read the vocabulary word from the passage and guess the meaning of each word from the context. Write the meaning of the word and then write a sentence using the word correctly.

1. affable

| Meaning: friendly |
| Sentence: We had a great conversation with a very affable group of people. |

2. affluent

| Meaning: |
| Sentence: |

3. afflicted

| Meaning: |
| Sentence: |

4. aqueous

Meaning:
Sentence:

5. arduous

Meaning:
Sentence:

6. agitated

Meaning:
Sentence:

7. after a spell

Meaning:
Sentence:

8. acquiesce

Meaning:
Sentence:

9. diligently

Meaning:
Sentence:

10. pretend

Meaning:
Sentence:

11. giggled

Meaning:
Sentence:

12. fond

| Meaning: |
| Sentence: |

13. turns out

| Meaning: |
| Sentence: |

14. proposed

| Meaning: |
| Sentence: |

D. FILL IN THE BLANK

Choose one of the appropriate vocabulary words to fill in the blanks. Remember to change the form if necessary.

propose	pretend	arduous
turn out	diligently	afflict
fond	acquiesce	affluent
giggle	after a spell	affable
	agitate	

1. I thought that my girlfriend and I were happy together, but it ____turned out____ that she wasn't happy, and she left me last week.

2. Every time I watch my father try to change my little brother's diaper, I _____ because it is obvious he doesn't know what he is doing.

3. John comes from a very _____ family. They own half of the real estate in Toronto.

4. My friend Peter is very _____, but girls think he is too nice, so he has a hard time finding a date.

5. Mary _____ studies her algebra notes every day until the test.

6. Sandra thought everyone was _____ of cats, but it turns out her neighbors don't like them at all.

7. Kent was studying, but _____ he met his friends to have a bite to eat.

8. Karen has to _____ that she is visiting my house when she visits her boyfriend because her parents are very strict.

9. All the cows on the farm are being watched by the federal government after several cows nearby were _____ with mad cow disease.

10. The hiking trip in the Canadian Rocky Mountains is going to be very _____; it's not for amateurs.

11. The criminal insisted that he was innocent, but when the jury said he was guilty and the police came to his home, he _____ and went with them without a word.

12. Mike and Tom don't get along, but as their friends, we have _____ a solution to help them stop their fighting. I hope they accept it.

13. Timmy lost $300 and looked _____ for the rest of the day.

Writing Activity

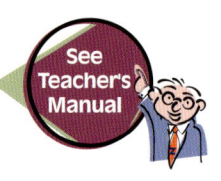

Read the story about Carmen one more time.
Imagine that ten years have passed in her life. What is she doing now? What is the situation with her and Tony? How is their life? Are they happy and content? Did they encounter obstacles in their married life? Did they have children?

_____
_____
_____
_____

Stand-Up Activity

Interview your partner and ask the following questions. Compare your preferences. How happy is the class in general?

1. If you were to go back in time, what would you change?

    - **a:** ☐ Nothing at all
    - **b:** ☐ Some things
    - **c:** ☐ Everything

2. If you won the lottery and had so much money to spare for vanity like plastic surgery, what part of your physical appearance would you change?

    - **a:** ☐ Nothing at all
    - **b:** ☐ Some parts

    c: ☐ Almost everything
    d: ☐ Everything

3. If your concept of a "perfect life" is having millions of dollars in savings and investment, living in a palatial house complete with household help, riding luxury chauffer-driven cars, traveling and vacationing in other countries when you feel like it, how close are you to attaining this "perfect life?"

    a: ☐ Very close
    b: ☐ Somewhat close
    c: ☐ Not at all close

4. Are you satisfied with your overall relationships with family, friends, or partner?

    a: ☐ Very satisfied
    b: ☐ Fairly satisfied
    c: ☐ Dissatisfied

5. Are you satisfied with your career choice, job, or profession?

    a: ☐ Very satisfied
    b: ☐ Fairly satisfied
    c: ☐ Neither satisfied nor dissatisfied

6. If you compare yourself to most people, how would you consider yourself?

    a: ☐ More fortunate
    b: ☐ Just as fortunate
    c: ☐ Less fortunate

7. How would you consider your outlook on life?

    a: ☐ Optimistic
    b: ☐ Pessimistic
    c: ☐ Somewhere in between

8. Do you set goals for yourself? How do you view them?

- **a:** ☐ Easy to achieve
- **b:** ☐ Challenging but achievable
- **c:** ☐ Very difficult to achieve
- **d:** ☐ I don't set goals for myself

9. What is your overall stress level?

- **a:** ☐ Low
- **b:** ☐ Moderate
- **c:** ☐ Fairly high
- **d:** ☐ Very high

10. In general, how satisfied are you with your life?

- **a:** ☐ Very satisfied
- **b:** ☐ Fairly satisfied
- **c:** ☐ Neither satisfied nor dissatisfied
- **d:** ☐ Dissatisfied

Check your responses. Each preference is one point.

ANALYSIS:

10 A's
You have managed to achieve a perfect balance in your life. Your positive outlook on life gives you a lot of strength. As a result, you feel less stress and more satisfaction than other people. In sum, you are a very happy person! Congratulations!

9 – 7 A's
Your personal goals closely match your internal beliefs, so you are mostly content and happy with what you have. You are happy, but desire to make some changes in your personal relationships and economic situation.

6 – 4 A's
You are usually happy, but you are unhappy with some aspects of your life. Focus on what you have, not just what you want to change. Making changes is good, but it's also important to recognize what you have.

3 – 1 A's
Maybe you need to think about making some changes in your life. You set goals for yourself, but you feel disappointed when you do not reach them. Take some time to write down where you want to be in one year, two years, and five years.

0 A's
You are not satisfied with your life at all. Think about talking more to your friends and family to help you with encouragement and support.

Lesson 14: Home is where the heart is

Pre-Reading Activity

GROUP WORK: Jigsaw
Work in groups. Discuss the following questions with your group and share your group's answers with the other groups in the class.

1. What would you do if you had everything in this world?

2. Was there ever a time when you were depressed or melancholic and did not know the exact reasons for your sadness?

3. Were you ever in a situation where you had to drop everything that you had been doing for many years and you decided to choose another path or career, or move to another country?

4. Do you think that you can play an important role in bringing happiness to other people? In what ways?

5. In many countries, having a pet is a standard practice. Do you think pets can make you happy?

Journal Writing

A. Write about a situation where you contributed to someone else's happiness or maybe sadness. Describe the person's reaction to your behavior.

MY JOURNAL

B. PAIR WORK

Exchange journals with a partner. Read your partner's journal and write a response to what your partner has written. Do you have different or similar experiences?

PARTNER'S RESPONSE

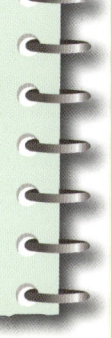

Interactive Reading

A. GROUP WORK: Each student reads a different paragraph. The rest of the class listens, and comprehends the story and the meanings of the boldfaced words.

NOBODY LOVES BUDDY

Buddy is a Golden Retriever that has lived in Union, New Jersey, his whole life. Buddy is a playful pet and likes to run, play, and **bark**. The house that he has lived in is not very big, but it has a yard, so Buddy doesn't mind so much; a small house and yard is better than living in the **dog pound**. Recently, Buddy has been **on edge** because he will soon be without an owner. His current owner is a retired army officer, who recently got married, and will be moving with his new wife to New York City. They will live in a small one-bedroom apartment on the Upper East

Side, and after much deliberation, they've decided that there just will not be enough room for Buddy. Buddy is nervous because if they can't find a home for him, they will take him to the dog pound. But Buddy knows that most people don't want to adopt large old dogs; they want cute little puppies. It's sad that most people only want to adopt puppies, because there are many dogs in pounds and **kennels** all over the world that would make wonderful pets. And there is no running and jumping at the dog pound. In fact, if you bark too loudly they tie your snout shut with a **muzzle**. Buddy has also heard that if you stay at the dog pound too long, they will **put you to sleep**.

That's why Buddy has been **somber** and **jittery** for most of the day. Every time he sees his owner, he **scurries** to a corner to hide and covers his eyes with his **paws**. With his eyes closed, he can hear footsteps coming closer to his hiding place. "Oh no," he thinks. "This is it for me." With his eyes still covered, Buddy tries to remember running in a green field chasing a **rooster**. It's the only thing that can calm him down.

Suddenly, Buddy's happy thoughts are interrupted by a soft whisper. "Hey there, fella," the **delicate** voice says. "How are you doing?" Buddy feels hands gently rubbing his neck and then scratching behind his ears. He slowly moves his paws away from his eyes and sees a man and three children smiling down at him. "Who are these people?" he thinks to himself. They rub his neck some more until Buddy realizes that he is no longer hiding in the corner of the room. "Could it be that these are the people who will take me to the dog pound? I had better get out of here!" Buddy barks his meanest bark and runs for the open door. He jumps through it into the yard and runs for freedom. Just before he is able to, his owner **nabs** him by the neck. Buddy is not going to give up. "If this is my last moment alive, then I'm going to fight with everything I've got," he barks. He shows his teeth. He struggles, but ultimately he is subdued. The youngest of the children comes up behind Buddy and looks deep into Buddy's eyes. The boy smiles and says, "You're just scared. I know you're a good dog." The father of the three children, Mr. Gates, talks to Buddy's owner, signs some papers, and then takes Buddy's leash. Buddy stands up. He has given up all **impulse** to fight. "Well, this is it," he thinks. Slowly Mr. Gates, his three kids, and Buddy walk out of the small yard and into their car. They have "doggy treats" waiting. Buddy eats a few and lies down in the backseat as the car starts. Eventually the **hum** of the car helps Buddy fall asleep.

Mr. Gates drives and daydreams about his life. The recent turn of events have left him a single parent raising three children. Through hard work and dedication he has built a successful business in the field of Information Technology. He is a self-made man who spends most of his time going to parties, making social appearances, and attending business meetings and conferences. Life does not always work out as we plan it, he thinks. He remembers that one day, as a child, when he went with his father and picked out a dog from his neighbor's litter. He had always wanted a dog. He is happy that he has been able to share this experience with his sons now, and thinks about how one day, each of them will do the same with their sons.

They arrive at their home in New Jersey. Suddenly, Buddy is awakened by a big bump in the road. He looks up and sees not the small houses, but trees. The car turns suddenly and stops. Buddy sits up and looks out of the window. It's a beautiful suburban house with a big **yard**. The car door opens, and Buddy jumps out and races around the yard. He is the happiest he has ever been. Mr. Gates and the children all begin running and chasing after Buddy. "Wow! Now I have friends, too," he thinks. Buddy and the kids run and play all day. It is the best day of his life. At night, sitting next to the beds of the three kids, Buddy barks at each of them, "Good night." The middle child turns off the light, and just before Buddy falls asleep, he thinks to himself, "I have never been this happy before. I hope I'm not dreaming."

B. PAIR WORK: Comprehension Questions
Answer the questions with complete sentences and discuss with your partner.

1. Where did Buddy live before he was adopted?

2. Who was Buddy's first owner?

3. What kind of dog is Buddy?

4. What does Buddy like to do?

5. Why is Buddy afraid to be placed in a dog pound?

6. Why does Buddy think that no one would adopt him?

7. What does Buddy think they want to do to him when he sees Mr. Gates and his three kids?

8. Where does Mr. Gates take Buddy?

C. Discover the Meaning
Match the given words with their correct meanings. Refer to the story for clues.

COLUMN A	COLUMN B
_o_ 1. dog pound	a. fragile; easily damaged
___ 2. bark	b. make a low, continuous, droning sound
___ 3. on edge	c. a device placed over an animal's mouth to prevent the animal from biting
___ 4. kennel	d. to catch, to take with force.
___ 5. put to sleep	e. extremely serious; grave; depressing
___ 6. somber	f. to kill an animal through injection

_____ 7. jittery

_____ 8. scurry

_____ 9. paws

_____ 10. rooster

_____ 11. delicate

_____ 12. nab

_____ 13. muzzle

_____ 14. impulse

_____ 15. hum

g. the sound a dog makes

h. to be nervous especially when expecting something bad

i. walking quickly

j. a male chicken

k. urge without thinking

l. the feet and hands of a dog

m. feeling anxious or nervous

n. shelter where you keep dogs

o. the place where abandoned dogs are kept

D. PAIR WORK

Reread the story about Buddy one more time and then place these sentences in the correct chronological order.

Pair Practice — See Teacher's Manual

a. Buddy hides because he thinks they will kill him.	f. Buddy runs around in a big yard and plays with children.
b. Mr. Gates takes Buddy to his home.	g. Buddy meets Mr. Gates and his three kids.
c. Buddy plays in the yard in Union, New Jersey.	h. Buddy has been somber and jittery for most of the day.
d. Mr. Gates drives and daydreams about his life.	i. The army officer is moving to New York City.
e. Buddy barks his meanest bark and runs for the open door.	j. Buddy lives happily with Mr Z and his kids.

1. (C) Buddy plays in the yard in Union, New Jersey.

2. _____

3. _____

4. _____

5. _____

6. _____

7. _____

8. _____

9. _____

10. _____

E. Conversation Practice

Write a dialogue between Mr. Gates or one of the children and Buddy. Use ten vocabulary words.

Mr. Gates:	Buddy, welcome to your new home.
Buddy:	Woof, Woof.
Mr. Gates:	Are you hungry?
Buddy:	
Mr. Gates:	
Buddy:	
Mr. Gates:	
Buddy:	
Mr. Gates:	

Buddy:

Mr. Gates:

Buddy:

Mr. Gates:

Buddy:

F. GROUP WORK: Vocabulary
Work with your group to write a sentence using the boldfaced words above.

1. **dog pound**

2. **bark**

3. **on edge**

4. **kennel**

5. **put to sleep**

6. **somber**

7. **jittery**

8. **scurry**

9. **paws**

10. **roosters**

11. **delicate**

12. **nab**

13. **muzzle**

14. **impulse**

15. **hum**

Lesson 15 — DON'T WORRY, BE HAPPY!

Pre-Reading Activity

GROUP WORK: Jigsaw
Work in groups. Discuss the following questions with your group and share your group's answers with the other groups in the class.

1. Have you ever taken something or someone for granted?

2. Which emotion is stronger: happiness or sadness?

3. Have you ever been blamed for someone else's problems?

4. Do you have regrets in life?

Journal Writing

A. Write about an experience in your life when everything went wrong.

MY JOURNAL

B. PAIR WORK

Exchange journals with a partner. Read your partner's journal and write a response to what your partner has written. Do you have different or similar experiences?

PARTNER'S RESPONSE

Interactive Reading

A. Each student reads a different paragraph. The rest of the class listens.

GUESS WHO'S DEPRESSED?

Dear Happiness,

Where have you been my whole life?

My name is Giuseppe Temporeli. I was born in a small **quaint** town in Italy. My mother and father were both charming schoolteachers. They loved me, their jobs, and the town where we lived, and they were always there to provide me with everything that I needed. They were happy, but I was not.

Let me explain why. I believe that my parents **perpetuated** the idea that it is fine not to be rich as long as you are happy, so I grew up deficient of all the skills one needs to become rich. I blame my parents for the fact that I live in a homeless shelter. Why can't I have an enormous three-bedroom apartment all to myself on New York's Park Avenue? Think I'm crazy? Well, I'll tell you one thing: Finding happiness is a **daunting** task, but if you've got money, at least you can buy it.

That's not the only reason why I blame my parents for my unhappiness. You might think this next reason is absurd, but before you judge me, listen. Because my parents were teachers, they forced me to study and do my homework every day.

They would help me every night. We would go over the **pertinent** information that I would need the next day in class. Instead of doing my homework, I **longed** to be outside with my friends getting into trouble. I was so jealous when my neighbor, who lived in the adjacent apartment, told me he had smoked a cigarette. We were only twelve years old, but he was cooler than me at that time. While he was doing cool things like smoking cigarettes and running away from the **truancy** police, I was always at home studying, or participating in an abundance of school activities. Learning to play the piano was boring and playing basketball, even though I'm too short was frustrating.

Can you see now why I'm not happy? So what if my friend has lung cancer now? At least he had a fun childhood. Because I studied so much, I graduated valedictorian of my high school. What a drag! I had to make a speech during graduation that had to **cater** to an **abundant** crowd of teachers, students, and parents. The night before, I was **feverishly** working on my speech while other students were getting drunk at a house party. The police arrested them for underage drinking, but who cares? That's the cool thing about high school. I mean, who hasn't gotten arrested in high school? Only nerds like me, I bet! I got a full scholarship to Harvard and felt miserable about it. I wanted to go to a cool "party school" somewhere in Ohio, and play football, drink, date cheerleaders, and wake up with a hangover. That is what college is all about, but it was not that for me. I studied hard again, graduated as valedictorian again, and had to give a speech again.

After graduation, a lot of companies wanted me to work for them, and I decided to work for a big investment bank in New York. They offered me a salary of $1 million a year. I was finally going to be rich.

On my first day, the **recession** hit New York City, and by the second day, I was **laid off**. When I told my parents, they only told me that it wasn't the end of the world and that they loved me. **Are you kidding me?** Without a job in New York City, my money **depleted** fast. My girlfriend left me because I didn't have a job. I became *adept* at shoplifting food and *toiletries* from the local drugstore. My parents urged me to return to Italy. They said my childhood friend Lara had returned and was single, beautiful, and successful. I talked to her on Facebook, and after three months, we decided to get married. We had been friends for a long time, and from the pictures I had seen of her, she was a real *looker*. She had long black hair and beautiful big brown eyes. I could not take my eyes off her *provocative* Facebook picture every night before I went to sleep.

My parents sent me a plane ticket, and everyone was waiting for me to return to Italy. While waiting for the gate agent to call my row for boarding, I went to the bookstore and tried to steal a magazine and some candy by stuffing them in my pants, but as I walked out of the store, I was stopped by a security guard. They held me in a small room for three hours, and finally I confessed to stealing. *Needless to say*, I missed my flight. None of this would have happened if my parents had never told me about Lara or bought me a ticket back to Italy. I served a painful twenty-four hours of community service at Central Park.

When I finished my community service, my mother and father were waiting for me. I looked at them and told them the truth—that I was very unhappy, that my life sucked, and that it was entirely their fault. I asked for $5 to take the bus and buy a lottery ticket, and that's what I'm doing now: waiting in line at the deli in front of the homeless shelter to buy a lottery ticket. As you can see, my future is bleak. So if you can hear me, happiness, I just want to ask: Where are you?

Thanks.

Sincerely,
Giuseppe

B. PAIR WORK: Comprehension Questions

Answer the questions with complete sentences and discuss with your partner.

1. Where is Giuseppe from?
2. Who does he blame for not being rich? Do you agree with him?
3. How was he able to go to college?
4. What does he wish he had done instead of studying in high school?
5. Are his parents good parents? Why?
6. Where does he live now?
7. In your opinion, do you think there is something wrong with Giuseppe?

C. PAIR WORK: Sentence Construction

Work with your partner to replace the boldfaced words with synonyms. Then use the words in sentences.

1. West Virginia is a state in the United States with an **abundance** of natural resources like coal.

   "West Virginia is a state in the United States with a lot of natural resources like coal.

2. Rita was sick yesterday. She had a **fever** of 102°F, so she took some medicine.

   _____

3. My friend is a **nerd** who studies all the time. It makes me angry because we never have fun together.

4. The magazine article was **provocative** because it explained the secrets of the fashion industry.

5. The **recession** is making it very difficult for small businesses to succeed.

6. I got **laid off** from my job because of excessive lateness.

7. **Are you kidding me?** You didn't really pay $30 for a cup of coffee, but if you did, they cheated you.

8. Kayla has been shopping all day, and now her money has been **depleted** so much that she can't buy anything to eat.

9. If you want to join the army, you should be in good physical health and **adept** at hand-to-hand combat.

10. If you want to make it through security at JFK airport, you have to carry very few **toiletries**, because if they are too big, or if you have too many, they will throw them away.

11. That girl is a real *looker*. She is so beautiful, but I'm too shy to go up and speak to her.

_____

12. I am a good person. ***Needless to say,*** I also have my faults like everyone else.

_____

13. Bryan loves his girlfriend and doesn't want to lose her, so for now, he *caters* to her every will.

_____

14. Timothy *longs* to go back to his country, but he has to finish studying at the University of Vancouver first.

_____

15. This magazine has *pertinent* information about future investments.

_____

16. Lara always thought that living in a big city was *absurd*, until she moved to New York and changed her mind.

_____

17. The children were having a fun time at the zoo when an *enormous* bear scared them, and they decided to never go to the zoo again.

_____

18. Marc is *deficient* in vitamins, so he needs to take a multivitamin supplement.

_____

19. When the president took office, he realized that the problems that faced the nation were **daunting**, but he was up to the task.

_____

20. When my best friend James gave a homeless man $20, it **perpetuated** the idea that he is rich, but he is not.

_____

21. The firemen were in such a hurry that they ran over my grandmother's cat. They tried to save it, but the outcome looked **bleak**.

_____

22. Our **quaint** house is so beautiful that everyone who passes by takes a picture of it.

_____

Assessment

Interview

Project

Develop a questionnaire of ten to fifteen questions about the concept of happiness, and interview people who you know are successful in life. Write an essay about the results of your interview and report it to the class. Write a brief background of your interviewee.

Grammar Review

A compound sentence is a sentence that joins together two separate clauses (idea, sentence, or statement) connected by a comma and a conjunction.

Examples:
- John eats a sandwich every day at work, but Tony doesn't like to eat at work.

Compound sentences are a great way to express similar or different ideas in the same sentence, depending on which conjunction is used to connect the sentences. Popular conjunctions are:

and	but	or	yet	so

A complex sentence is a sentence that has two independent ideas that have a direct relationship to each other. Usually these ideas are joined by a connector.

Examples:
- Anthony has eaten a sandwich every day since he moved to Vancouver.

The two ideas are joined together by a connector. Some popular connectors are:

after	as	before	since	until
when	while	because	if	although

Glossary

Vocabulary Word	Part of Speech	Pronunciation	Meaning
absurd	adjective	[ab-**surd**]	utterly or obviously senseless, illogical, or untrue
abundant	adjective	[*uh*-**buhn**-d*uh*nt]	present in great quantity
acquiesce	verb	[ak-wee-es]	to submit or comply silently or without protest
adept	adjective	[uh-**dept**]	very skilled; proficient; expert
affable	adjective	[**af**-uh-buhl]	pleasantly easy to approach and to talk to
afflicted	adjective	[uh-**flik**-tid]	to be sick with mental or bodily pain
affluent	adjective	[**af**-loo-uhnt]	having an abundance of wealth, property, or other material goods; prosperous; rich
after a spell	idiom	[**af**-te]r [*uh*] [*spel*]	after some time has passed
agitated	adjective	[**aj**-i-tey-tid]	excited; disturbed

Word	Part of Speech	Pronunciation	Definition
amass	verb	[uh-**mas**]	to collect into a mass or pile; gather
aqueous	adjective	[**ey-k**wee-uhs]	of, like, or containing water; watery
arduous	adjective	[**ahr**-joo-uhs]	difficult, requiring great exertion
Are you kidding me?	idiom	[ahr] [yoo] [kidding] [mee]	Please tell the truth; are you serious
bark	noun/verb	[bahrk]	the sound dogs make
bereft	adjective	[bih-**reft**]	deprived of
bleak	adjective	[bleek]	bare, desolate, and often windswept
break down	idiom	[breyk] [doun]	can be simplified into basic parts
catalyst	noun	[**kat**-l-ist]	something that causes something else to happen quickly, without itself being affected
characterize	verb	[**kar-ik**-tuh-rahyz]	to mark or distinguish as a quality
companionship	noun	[kuhm-**pan**-yuhn-ship]	association as companions; fellowship
contentment	noun	[kuhn-**tent**-muhnt]	satisfaction; ease of mind
criterion	noun	[krahy-**teer**-ee-uhn]	a standard of judgment or criticism
daunting	adjective	[**dawn**-ting]	intimidating; overwhelming with fear
de facto	idiom	[dee **fak**-toh]	in fact; in reality; by default
deficient	adjective	[dih-**fish**-uhnt]	lacking some element or characteristic
delicate	adjective	[**del**-i-kit]	gentile, fragile
deplete	adjective	[dih-**pleet**]	to be decreased
diligently	adverb	[**dil**-i-juhnt]	attentive and persistent in doing anything
dog pound	noun	[dog] [pound]	a public enclosure for stray or unlicensed dogs
endeavors	noun	[en-**dev**-er]	a determined effort
enormous	adjective	[**ih**-nawr-muhs]	huge; immense
fascination	noun	[fas-uh-**ney**-shuhn]	the state or an instance of being very interested in something
feverish	adjective	[**fee**-ver-ish]	excited, restless, or uncontrolled
be fond of	idiom	[fond]	to like something
fortunate	adjective	[**fawr**-ch*uh*-nit]	lucky
giggle	verb	[**gig**-uhl]	to laugh in a silly, often high-pitched way
hierarchy	noun	[**hahy**-uh-rahr-kee]	any system of persons or things ranked one above another
hum	noun/verb	[huhm]	a low, continuous, droning sound
impulse	noun	[**im**-puhls]	sudden, involuntary inclination prompting to action
jittery	adjective	[**jit**-uh-ree]	extremely tense and nervous
kennel	noun	[**ken**-l]	a house or shelter for a dog or a cat
long for	idiom	[lawng] [fawr]	to have an earnest or strong desire or craving
looker	idiom	[**loo k**-er]	a good-looking person

Word	Part of Speech	Pronunciation	Definition
muzzle	noun/verb	[**muhz**-uh l]	a device placed over an animal's mouth to prevent the animal from biting
nab	verb	[nap]	to grab, seize suddenly
needless to say	idiom	[**need**-lis] [too] [sey]	something understood easily; no explanation is necessary
nerd	noun	[nurd]	an intelligent but single-minded person obsessed with a nonsocial hobby or pursuit
on edge	idiom	[on] [ej]	to be nervous especially when expecting something bad
paw	noun	[paw]	the foot of an animal with claws
perceive	verb	[per-**seev**]	to become aware of, know, or identify by means of the senses
perpetuate	verb	[per-**pech**-oo-eyt]	to keep something going over a long period of time
persecute	verb	[**pur**-si-kyoot]	to pursue with harassing or oppressive treatment
pertinent	adjective	[**pur**-tn-uhnt]	important, relevant
plagued	adjective	[**pleyg**-d]	to be afflicted with or persistently annoyed by
pretend	verb	[pri-**tend**]	to appear falsely, to deceive
propose	verb	[pruh-**pohzd**]	offer, suggest
provocative	adjective	[pruh-**vok**-uh-tiv]	causing a strong reaction
pursue	verb	[per-**soo**]	to follow close upon; go with; attend
put (an animal) to sleep	idiom	[poot] [an][**an**-uh-muhl][to] [sleep]	kill a sick, old or abandoned animal in a humane way
quaint	adjective	[kweynt]	having an old-fashioned attractiveness or charm; picturesque
qualify	verb	[**kwol**-uh-fahy]	to provide with proper or necessary skills, knowledge, credentials
quantify	verb	[**kwon**-tuh-fahy]	to determine, indicate, or express the quantity of.
recession	noun	[ri-**sesh**-uhn]	a period of economic decrease
rooster	noun	[**roo**-ster]	a male chicken
scurry	verb	[**skur**-ee]	to go or move quickly or in haste.
somber	adjective	[**som**-ber]	gloomy dark; sad
subjective	adjective	[suhb-**jek**-tiv]	existing in the mind; belonging to the thinking subject rather than to the object of thought
to no avail	idiom	[too] [**noh**] [uh-**veyl**]	of no use or advantage
toiletry	noun	[**toi**-li-tree]	any article or preparation used in cleaning or grooming oneself
turn out	idiom	[turnz] [out]	surprising end result
yard	noun	[yahrd]	the large area in front or behind a house

Source: Dictionary.com

UNIT 5

CONSUMERISM

"Caveat Emptor"
(Let the buyer beware.)
—Anonymous, 1523

Info tip:
Some 12 percent of the world's population lives in North America and Western Europe, and accounts for 60 percent of private consumption spending, but a third of humanity living in South Asia and sub-Saharan Africa account for only 3.2 percent.

Source: World Watch Institute

Lesson 16: What is Consumerism?

Pre-Reading Activity

GROUP WORK: Jigsaw
Work in groups. Discuss the following questions with your group and share your group's answers with the other groups in the class.

See Teacher's Manual

1. Look at the pictures above. What did the person receive in the first picture?

2. Have you received such "special offers" from scam artists enticing you to buy products?

3. What do you think of this marketing ploy?

4. How often do you go shopping? What do you usually buy?

5. Do you pay in cash or credit? Why?

6. What things do you take into consideration when you are buying a product: price, quality, or brand name?

7. Who are more of impulsive shoppers: men or women?

Journal Writing

A. Write about a product and a brand that you can't live without. Refer to the questions.

- √ What is it? Describe its features.
- √ Where and when did you get it?
- √ Why did you buy it?
- √ How often do you use it?
- √ What would you do if you lost it?

MY JOURNAL

B. PAIR WORK

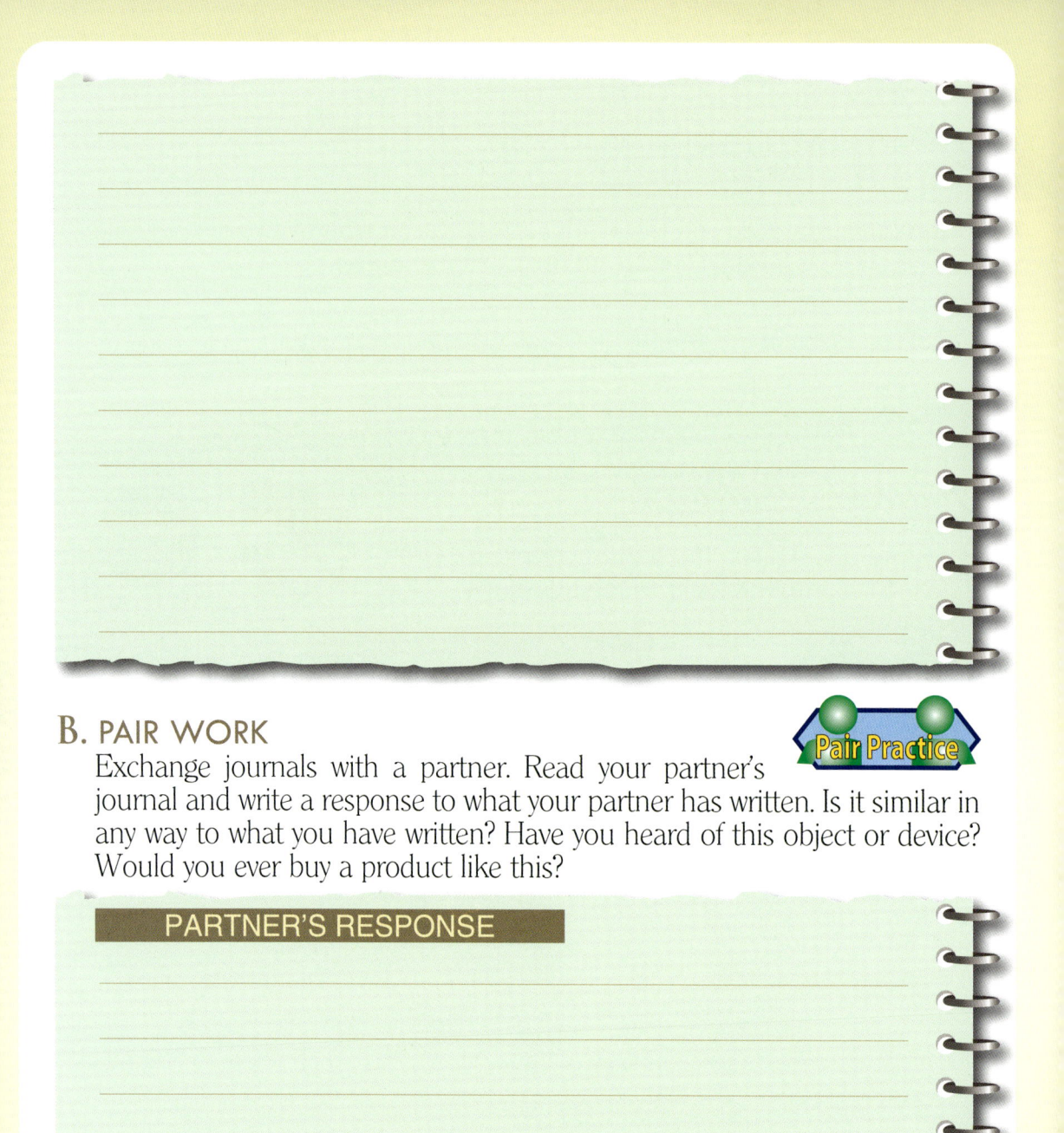

Exchange journals with a partner. Read your partner's journal and write a response to what your partner has written. Is it similar in any way to what you have written? Have you heard of this object or device? Would you ever buy a product like this?

PARTNER'S RESPONSE

Reading Exercise 1

A. Read with your group to find the definitions for the boldfaced words and put a one-word synonym in the box. Use contextual clues to understand the meaning of the words.

WHAT IS CONSUMERISM?

How long is the **warranty**[1] good for on my computer, washer, dryer, or cell phone? Will it last for five years? Which product is better? Will I **get my money's worth**[2] out of this? Is it better to buy many cheap products or one good, expensive item? Does it taste good? Is it as fresh as it should be? Is it safe to eat? Will this drug harm my health or the health of my family? Am I buying this product because I need it or because I just want it?

These are some of the questions that most people ask **on a regular basis**[3] before they make a purchase. These consumer questions **reflect**[4] people's feelings about how they spend their money, the **relative**[5] value of what they purchase, and their worries about the health and **welfare**[6] of themselves and their families. The concept of

Synonyms

1. _____
2. _____
3. _____
4. _____
5. _____
6. _____

consumerism evolved as a *response*[7] to people's concerns about the value and safety of what they buy. It is also related to people's buying behavior of essential and nonessential goods and services depending on the quality of the product and the effectiveness of its marketing and advertising strategies.

In the United States, there are several *agencies*[8] that *regulate*[9] the products that are manufactured and sold as well as the food raised and grown, and the drugs produced and sold in the country—the Federal Trade Commission (FTC), the Food and Drug Administration (FDA) and the National Highway Traffic Safety Administration (NHTSA). These government groups seek to *ensure*[10] that companies produce safe products. In addition, each year the US Congress passes *legislation*[11] regulating the food we eat, the drugs we take, the cars we drive, the household cleansers we use, and anything else that might affect consumers' lives. Also, the Consumer Protection Agency, part of the FTC, is an organization set up to protect consumers from "unfair business practices" and from being sold products and services that are, according to the agency's Web site, "fraudulent and deceptive."

Consumers can go to the Consumer Protection Agency's Web site to find out about how to protect themselves from identity theft and the latest *schemes*[12] or *scams*[13] that criminals use to convince consumers to hand over their money in return for inferior, or possibly nonexistent, products and services. Consumers can also *file a complaint*[14] with the agency against a company they feel has taken advantage of them.

7. _____
8. _____
9. _____
10. _____
11. _____
12. _____
13. _____
14. _____

In addition to governmental agencies, the Consumer Union publishes a magazine called *Consumer Reports*, which evaluates the quality of products and services. They cover everything from coffee quality and taste to the best buy for a mobile phone plan.

15. _____
16. _____
17. _____

In May 2009, President Barack Obama signed into law the Credit Card ***Accountability***[15], Responsibility, and ***Disclosure***[16] Act, which will protect consumers from unfair practices of credit card companies. The bill includes a ban on interest rate increases on balances previously owed on cards. In addition, it requires companies to provide at least twenty-one days for account holders to pay the bill from the time of the bill being mailed. It also ends "late fee traps" in which deadlines for payments fall on a weekend, fall in the middle of the day, and prevents ***deadline***[17] dates from changing from month to month. These and other parts of the law will not only help consumers manage their bills but also keep credit available for people and the US economy.

So the question is, How do you protect yourself and your family from poorly made products, bad services, or other hazards of living in the modern world? Do you think you are responsible for conducting research for the right product or refund policies before buying? Do you think the government should allow more competition to force companies to improve their products and services? Do you think it is better to have more regulations than a free market, or vice versa?

B. PAIR WORK: Comprehension Questions

Answer the questions with complete sentences and discuss with your partner. Exchange your answers with other pairs in the class; then check as a group.

1. What is consumerism?

   _____
   _____

2. What three governmental agencies regulate products in the United States?

   _____

3. What part of the FTC is concerned with consumer fraud?

   _____

4. How can consumers find out about products and services that may possibly harm them?

   _____

5. What is the name of the magazine that consumers can use to find out about product ratings?

   _____

6. In your opinion, are you an educated consumer? If so, why? If not, why not?

   _____

C. SKIMMING FOR MAIN IDEAS

Write the main idea of the article and two details which support the main idea.

See Teacher's Manual

MAIN IDEA

_____

_____

TWO SUPPORTING DETAILS OF THE MAIN IDEA

1. _____
2. _____

D. PAIR WORK

Write a sentence using the boldfaced words from the reading passage.

1. **warranty**

2. **get my money's worth**

3. **on a regular basis**

4. **reflect**

5. relative (to)

6. welfare

7. response

8. agencies

9. regulate

10. ensure

11. legislation

12. scheme

13. scam

14. file a complaint

15. **accountability**

16. **disclosure**

17. **deadline**

Writing Activity
Internet Research

Do research on the Internet about a product or service you have recently purchased or heard about. What factors have led you to buy the product? Find out what the opinions of other buyers are and what information the consumer protection agency provides on this product, or look at the agency's section on consumer information, and choose an area that interests you. Take notes on what you find. Then present your findings to the class.

Example: You are researching about your iPhone. You may type in Google.

Google

iPhone reviews

Google Search | I'm feeling lucky.

Reading Exercise 2

A. Read with your group to find the definitions for the boldfaced words and put a one-word synonym in the box. Use contextual clues to understand the meaning of the words.

What Is the Price of a Karaoke Machine?

"I'd love to be there, Mom, but I can't tonight," Alicia called from the back bedroom. "I just got a text from Jee Young. She wants to meet at 8 p.m. We're going shopping."

"Humph." Justine took the plates from the cabinet. "Where is she getting the money to go shopping?" Justine wondered. "That's her college money. Doesn't she know ***money doesn't grow on trees***[1]?"

"You'll miss dinner if you go out now. Grandma and Grandpa are coming. They're bringing dessert from the old neighborhood. Can't you put it off till tomorrow?" ***Convincing***[2] Alicia to be at home when family came over had become nearly impossible since she started to work. All she wanted to do was shop—clothes, shoes, compact discs, smartphones. Technology and fashion had replaced family meals and card games. Where did the girl get it from?

"Mom," said Alicia, breathless from rushing around the house, when she entered the kitchen. "There's a big sale at the mall. I ***absolutely***[3] have to get there. All the girls are wearing UGGs this winter, and I have to get a pair. I'll be back."

Synonyms

1. _____
2. _____
3. _____

She **charged**[4] toward the door but was **intercepted**[5] by her mother's arm across the doorway. "How much have you **put away**[6] this week?"

"Put away?" Alicia asked innocently.

"You know what I mean. You are supposed to be saving for college."

"I am, Mom. Besides, if I don't have enough money for college, I can just apply for **financial aid**[7] and government loans. Everybody does it."

"Alicia," Justine leaned in toward her daughter. "Don't spend your whole paycheck on these boots. Show some **restraint**[8]. Saving money is a good habit, and spending everything you earn is a bad one. You can't count on government loans and financial aid to get through college or life. You have to have your own money."

"Oh, Mom, you just don't understand. This is a really big sale, and I just won't feel right if I don't have them this winter. I had to go the whole of last year with those." She pointed to the green **rubberized**[9] boots in the corner of the kitchen.

"They were enough for last year, right? They kept your feet warm and dry, and **held up**[10] for more than one season. They were a good buy." Justine moved her arm away from the doorway and crossed them across her chest.

"Mom, not everything is about a good buy. Some things are about enjoyment."

"Be back in time for dinner with your grandparents," Justine sighed as Alicia **planted**[11] a kiss on her mother's cheek and **dashed**[12] out of the apartment.

Justine thought about what Alicia had said. Maybe she was right. Maybe sometimes it's good to just spend money for enjoyment. Maybe she was being too **prudent**[13].

The jiggling of the front door handle jogged her out of her thoughts. "It

4. _____
5. _____
6. _____
7. _____
8. _____
9. _____
10. _____
11. _____
12. _____
13. _____

must be Roger home from work already." She **glanced**[14] at the clock. It was later than she'd thought. "Why is he so late?"

"Hey," Roger yelled from the doorway. "Where is everybody?"

"I'm in the kitchen. The roast is almost done, and your parents will be here in twenty minutes. Why are you so late?" Justine **poked**[15] her head out of the kitchen in time to see Roger slipping into the living room with a big box in his arms.

"What's in the box?" Justine asked cautiously. She **slid**[16] down the hallway and **peered**[17] into the living room.

14. _____
15. _____
16. _____
17. _____
18. _____
19. _____
20. _____
21. _____
22. _____
23. _____

Roger was unpacking what happened to be a karaoke machine. "Isn't it great? It was on sale at the mall." He **grinned triumphantly**[18] at Justine. "We'll use it tonight with Mom and Dad."

"Don't mean to **burst your bubble**[19], darling, but how much did that cost?" Was it possible that she would have to have the same conversation with a grown man that she had just had with a sixteen-year-old girl?

"It wasn't that much." He slid the machine out of the box and placed it on top of the coffee table. I've been doing a lot of **overtime**[20] lately, and I thought that it would be something fun for the family to do in the evenings together. Besides, what's money for if not for some fun?"

"It's fine." Justine's tone was **resigned**[21]. "It's just that I had a similar conversation with Alicia about spending money on **frivolous**[22] purchases and not saving enough for the future. I just worry about the lessons we're teaching our daughter."

"Honey, we do save. I save, you save, and Alicia, well, she isn't a compulsive buyer." His tone was **soothing**[23]. We're not going broke over this. It's all about balance." He put his arm around her shoulders.

"I suppose so." Justine looked up at him and smiled. "Maybe we just have to make good choices all around."

Roger leaned in to kiss her forehead just as the oven buzzer went off in the kitchen and the front doorbell rang.

"My roast!" exclaimed Justine.

"My parents!" said Roger, as they each ran off in opposite directions.

B. PAIR WORK: Comprehension Questions
Answer the following questions in complete sentences based on the story above.

1. What is Justine doing at the beginning of the story?

2. Why isn't Alicia going to be at home that evening?

3. How does Alicia plan to spend her paycheck?

4. Why is Justine concerned about her daughter's behavior?

5. Why do you think Alicia doesn't like the green boots?

6. How does Justine react when Roger comes home?

7. Why did Roger buy the karaoke machine?

8. Why is Justine worried about Roger's purchase?

9. What is their important decision at the end of the story?

10. What is the significance of the title?

11. Do you think Americans and Canadians are impulsive shoppers? How about the people in your country?

C. GROUP WORK: Vocabulary

Work with your group to write a sentence using the vocabulary words.

1. money doesn't grow on trees

2. convincing

3. absolutely

4. charged

5. intercepted

6. put away

7. restraint

8. rubberized

9. held up

10. planted

11. dashed

12. **prudent**

13. **glanced**

14. **poked**

15. **slid**

16. **peered**

17. **grinned**

18. **triumphantly**

19. **burst your bubble**

20. **overtime**

21. **resigned**

22. **frivolous**

23. **soothing**

Lesson 17
COMPARING OPINIONS

Pre-Reading Activity

GROUP WORK: Jigsaw

Work in groups. Discuss the following questions with your group and share your group's answers with the other groups in the class.

Group Work

JIGSAW

See Teacher's Manual

1. What are the people in the pictures doing?

2. How do you decide which product to buy when you have to choose between two similar products?

3. What do you do when something you have bought doesn't work anymore?

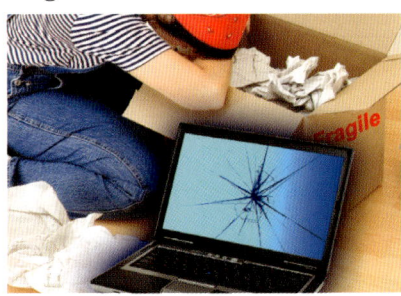

4. What differences have you noticed about the way product failure is dealt with in the United States or Canada and the way it is dealt with in your country?

5. Have you ever returned a product that you were dissatisfied with? How many times?

Journal Writing

A. Write about a product that you would like to buy but can't afford. Refer to the questions.

See Teacher's Manual

- √ What is the product?
- √ Describe its features.
- √ Do other people like it?
- √ What would you do with it?
- √ Do you really need it or are you following a trend?
- √ What do you think about the products sold in discount stores or flea markets? Are they worth buying?

MY JOURNAL

B. PAIR WORK

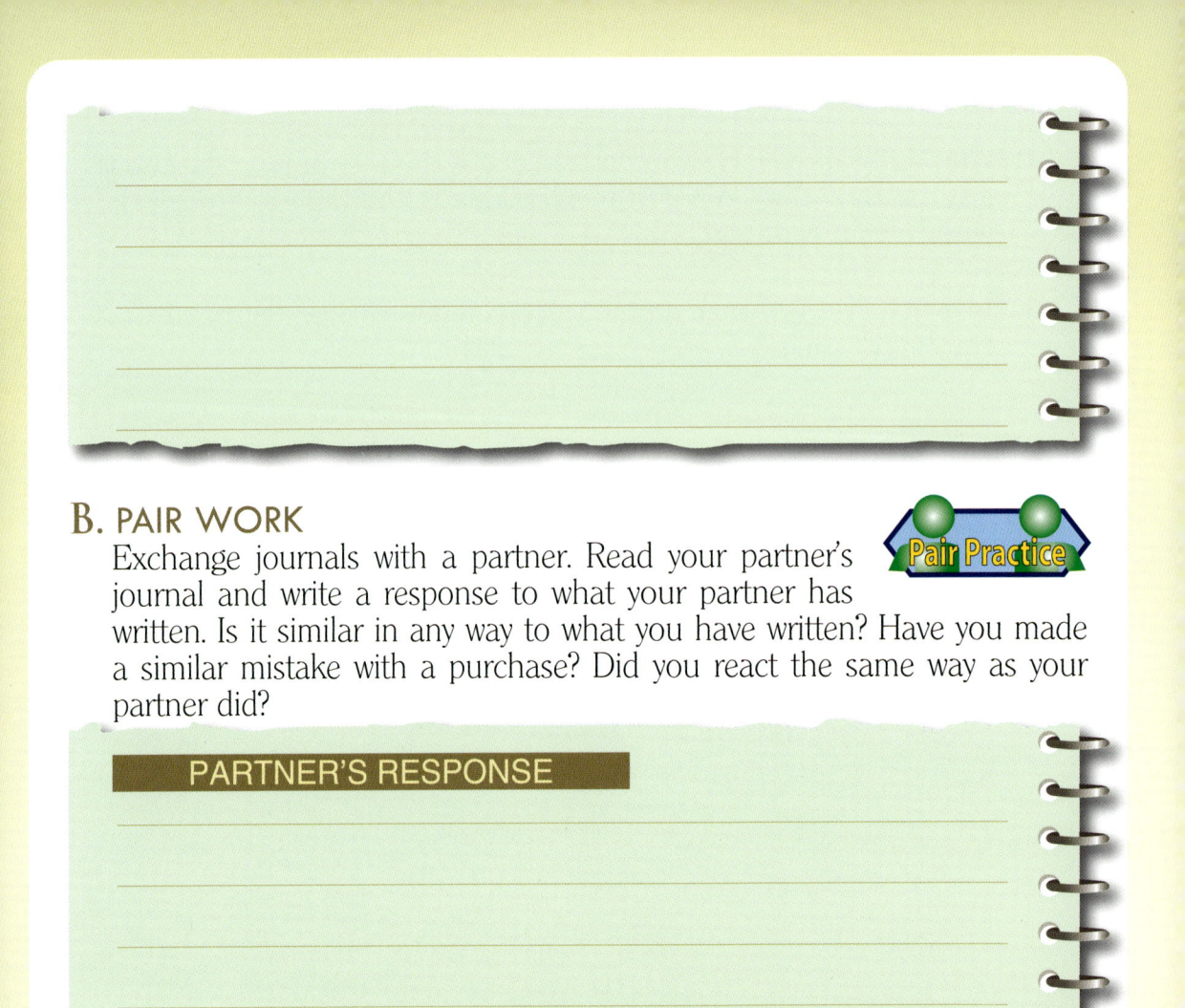

Exchange journals with a partner. Read your partner's journal and write a response to what your partner has written. Is it similar in any way to what you have written? Have you made a similar mistake with a purchase? Did you react the same way as your partner did?

PARTNER'S RESPONSE

Reading Exercise

A. ROLE PLAY/GROUP WORK

Read the dialogue with your group to find the definitions for the boldfaced words and put a one-word synonym in the box. Use contextual clues to understand the meaning of the words.

ZONI RADIO

Moderator: The latest piece of technology has just come along the information highway, and here today to present the **merits**[1] and **detriments**[2] of this amazing new phone are the Technology Guys. Good morning, Russ. Good morning, Hugh. How are you this morning?

Hugh: Good, thanks.

Russ: Fine, thanks.

Moderator: So we have the latest product from ZYX Technologies. They just keep coming up with better and better stuff, don't they?

Hugh: Yeah. I've been in this business for twenty years, and I can say that I've never seen such a complete package in a phone before.

Russ: It is a remarkable device, that's for sure. But I have some **misgivings**[3] about it. But we'll get to that later. It's definitely not just for calling people.

Moderator: So let's get down to basics. What's good about this phone?

Hugh: Well, it's amazing. It's got all the **trappings**[4] of a phone: voice recorder, messaging/texting, Internet data capabilities. And all of these are great. It has a clear display. The voice quality is **as clear as a bell**[5], even in areas that were previously known as **dead zones**[6].

Russ: Which is a **testament**[7] to the unbelievable service that ZYX provides its users.

Hugh: And of course, it has GPS navigation and a 12-megapixel camera.

Russ: So you can get the absolute clearest picture of just about anything you photograph with or without good background lighting.

Hugh: And it includes both a keyboard, with your regular buttons, and a touch screen function.

Moderator: So it combines the best of the latest technology and caters[8] to both user preferences[9].

Hugh: Exactly, but that is not all it can do.

Moderator: What else can it do?

Hugh: Well, it can put on a slide-show presentation that you have downloaded from your computer and stored on its Super X memory. It can take readings from the environment to detect **toxins**[10] in the air. If you pass it over any living thing, it can sense what kind of thing it is and give you an explanation of what it is, what it eats, where it **originates**[11] from, and pretty much anything else you want to know about it.

Moderator: That's amazing. So what's the **downside**[12]?

Synonyms

1. _____
2. _____
3. _____
4. _____
5. _____
6. _____
7. _____
8. _____
9. _____
10. _____
11. _____

Russ: That's where I come in. I'm afraid that there are some **drawbacks**[13] to this phone. The first one is the price. Right now it's more expensive than any other phone on the market by at least 30 percent.

Moderator: Ooh, that's a lot.

Russ: Yeah, and despite trying to make it pocket size, it barely fits in a large knapsack. It weighs about ten pounds.

Moderator: That's a lot to carry around.

Russ: And the battery life is really short. You can barely get through the day on one charge.

Moderator: Again, ouch.

Russ: So it's really **unfeasible**[14] to use on a daily basis. And although it has many great applications, do we really need a scanner that **detects**[15] toxins in the air, or can identify what kind of bug is lying on the ground?

Hugh: For those who work in **industries**[16] where pollutants are produced, I would say that it's completely appropriate.

Russ: Well, that's **neither here nor there**[17] because it would be too heavy to carry around and too **bulky**[18] to use.

Hugh: The benefits **outweigh**[19] the detriments.

Russ: We'll see about that.

Moderator: Ok, you guys. Let's break it up now. That's it for the two Technology Guys today. Next time the products we will be discussing are smoke detectors that read minds.

11. _____
12. _____
13. _____
14. _____
15. _____
16. _____
17. _____
18. _____
19. _____

B. PAIR WORK: Comprehension Questions
Answer the questions with complete sentences and discuss with your partner.

1. What is the latest product of ZYX Technologies?

   _____

   _____

2. What are the features of the new phone?

   _____

   _____

3. What is GPS?

   _____

   _____

4. What are the drawbacks of the phone?

   _____

   _____

C. GROUP WORK: Vocabulary
Work with your group to write a sentence using the boldfaced words above.

1. **merits**

2. **detriments**

3. misgivings

4. trappings

5. as clear as a bell

6. dead zone

7. testament

8. caters

9. preferences

10. toxins

11. originates

12. downside

13. drawbacks

14. unfeasible

15. detects

16. industries

17. neither here nor there

18. bulky

19. outweigh

D. PAIR WORK: Comparing Opinions

In the discussion about the latest piece of technology, the Technology Guys voice two different opinions about the latest phone from ZYX Technologies. In the table below, put the benefits and detriments into the two columns under the Technology Guys' names. You may add your own opinions about the latest technologies.

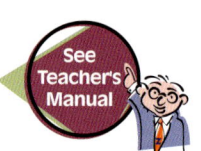

	Hugh	Russ
Benefits		
Detriments		

E. Vocabulary Expansion

Read each sentence and fill in the correct vocabulary word. Use each vocabulary word just once.

trappings	originated	industry
clear as a bell	downside	neither here nor there
dead zone	drawback	bulky
testament	unfeasible	outweigh
caters	detect	detriment
preferences	toxin	

1. I can't see any __detriment__ to having a new cell phone every year.

2. The car _____ uses computers to control speed and fuel usage instead of simple mechanics.

3. Their good behavior is a _____ to their good upbringing.

4. That vacation has all the _____ of a good time.

5. It's _____ whether you get the new phone or not. You still won't be able to call the moon.

6. We could understand every word he said because the reception was _____.

7. My cell phone doesn't work downtown because it's a _____ down there.

8. We have invented a device that can _____ whether or not a student has done his homework without even looking at the page.

9. This is a very new technology that _____ in another country.

10. This restaurant _____ to people who don't eat meat.

11. The new computers today are light and easy to carry, not _____ like those from several years ago.

12. There are a lot of good features on in this cell phone, but the one _____ is that the battery doesn't last.

13. The _____ in the water made it undrinkable.

14. It's just _____ to have every possible application on one phone. One would probably interfere with another.

15. I think that it's worth the money. The benefits definitely _____ the _____.

16. Most cell phones let you set your own user _____ when it comes to ringtones and background colors.

What Would You Say?

See Teacher's Manual

Work with your partner(s). Read the situations. For each situation, write what you would say using the vocabulary words.

1. Your friend has bought a product that doesn't work. He didn't get a warranty from the store.

    (Cabdy): I bought a new cell phone but it doesn't work. It drops calls in **dead zones**.

    (Ozge): That shouldn't be a problem. What does your warranty say?

(Cabdy): It doesn't *cater to* this kind of problem.

(Ozg): Then I think if it's *unfeasible,* to fix the problem, you should buy a new one.

2. You are trying to get the best buy on a new bluetooth headphones and want to ask the salesperson several questions.

(   ): _____

(   ): _____

(   ): _____

(   ): _____

3. You want to return a product to the store you got it from because it wasn't what you expected.

(   ): _____

(   ): _____

(   ): _____

(   ): _____

4. You are thinking of recommending a product that you like very much to a friend of yours.

(   ): _____

(   ): _____

(   ): _____

(   ): _____

Writing Activity
Analyzing a Product

GROUP WORK
Choose a technological product that everyone in your group is familiar with (cell phone, laptop, translator, tablet). Do research on the product and the various brands that produce that specific product and create a presentation in which you evaluate those brands. The rest of the class should take notes on what the presenters say about the product. Then discuss in groups which brand is best. The class should vote on the best brand for each group.

Lesson 18
Public Opinion Surveys: What Do Consumers Want?

Pre-Reading Activity

GROUP WORK: Jigsaw

Work in groups. Discuss the following questions with your group and share your group's answers with the other groups in the class.

1. What do the first and second pictures show?

2. Have you ever participated in a public opinion survey?

3. Do you think advertising influences consumer purchases?

4. What is the difference between the ways products are advertised in your homeland and the way products are advertised in the United States and Canada?

5. Do you think it is fair for advertisers to criticize products of other companies? Why or why not?

6. What has the strongest influence on purchases: price, packaging, or brand?

7. Are people willing to pay more for a product if they think they are getting more, even if it is beyond their budget?

Journal Writing

A. Write about a commercial that you have seen recently that has influenced a purchase you've made. Refer to the questions.

- ✓ What was the commercial for?
- ✓ Where did you see it?
- ✓ What happened in the commercial?
- ✓ Why do you think it had an influence on you?
- ✓ Did you really need the product or not? If so, for what purpose did you need it?

MY JOURNAL

B. PAIR WORK

Exchange journals with a partner. Read your partner's journal and write a response to what your partner has written. Is it similar in any way to what you have written? Have you made a similar mistake with a purchase? Did you react the same way as your partner did?

PARTNER'S RESPONSE

_____
_____
_____
_____

Reading Exercise

A. PAIR WORK

Read the passage below about how a survey is conducted and analyzed.

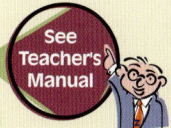

SURVEY ON SMART PHONES

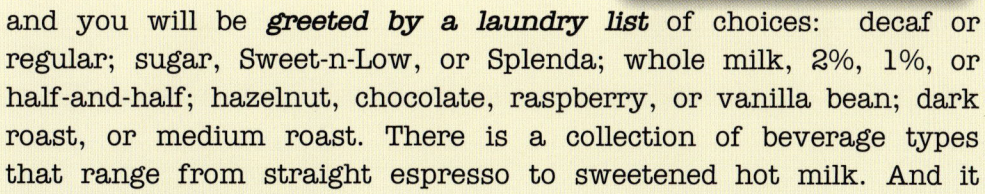

Today, there are more choices available to people than ever before. It *goes well beyond* Coke vs. Pepsi these days. Walk into any coffee shop and you will be *greeted by a laundry list* of choices: decaf or regular; sugar, Sweet-n-Low, or Splenda; whole milk, 2%, 1%, or half-and-half; hazelnut, chocolate, raspberry, or vanilla bean; dark roast, or medium roast. There is a collection of beverage types that range from straight espresso to sweetened hot milk. And it doesn't end there. We are asked to choose cell phones, carriers, packages, insurance policies, fast-food restaurants, and sneakers in every color of the rainbow. The *list goes on and on*.

Consumer purchases are influenced by many factors, including gender, age, ethnicity, and national origin. For our survey, we attempted to simply find out what the most important purchases people made in 2008 were and if there was any **correlation** between their age, ethnicity, or gender. We asked three questions about their preferences and three questions about *demographics**.

Our first question was about the three most important purchases they made last year. They had to check three choices from among the five products:

- **a:** ☐ smartphone
- **b:** ☐ plasma TV
- **c:** ☐ digital camera
- **d:** ☐ laptop computer (latest model)
- **e:** ☐ car

The second question was about what made them purchase their particular phone. They had five choices:

- **a:** ☐ advertisement
- **b:** ☐ friend's recommendation
- **c:** ☐ company's reputation
- **d:** ☐ appealing packaging
- **e:** ☐ discounts

The third question was related to whether they were satisfied with their purchase. Then once again they had five choices:

a: ☐ very satisfied
b: ☐ satisfied
c: ☐ somewhat satisfied
d: ☐ dissatisfied
e: ☐ extremely dissatisfied

Gender	Age Range	General Ethnic Background
a. male **b.** female	**a.** 18–25 **b.** 26–35 **c.** 36–45 **d.** 46–55 **e.** 55 and older	**a.** Asian **b.** African **c.** Native American **d.** Caucasian **e.** Hispanic or Latino

FINDINGS:

The findings were not that surprising. More than half the respondents had purchased a smartphone in 2017. Two-thirds of those who had purchased a smartphone were very satisfied with their purchases, while the remaining one-third were split between satisfied and very dissatisfied. Most of the respondents were between 18 and 25 years old. Their ethnicity seemed to have no effect on whether a consumer chose a cell phone or a smartphone. What was most interesting was that none of the respondents in the 55 and older category had a smartphone—they all had simple cell phones.

*Characteristics used to classify people for statistical purposes including but not limited to age, race, gender, ethnic origins, religion, and the like.

B. GROUP WORK : Vocabulary in Context

Work with your group to write definitions of the vocabulary words or expressions in context below.

1. His interest in ancient history **goes well beyond** looking at ancient pots in museums. He has begun to learn ancient languages.
   _____
   _____

2. When we entered the office, we were **greeted by** a pleasant receptionist who was happy to assist us.
   _____
   _____

3. She has a **laundry list of tasks** to do before she goes on vacation. She may not finish until she's ready to get on the plane.
   _____
   _____

4. The list of things for her to do **goes on and on**.
   _____
   _____

5. There may be a **correlation** between how tall one is and how high a person's self-esteem is, but height does not necessarily cause people to have good self-esteem.
   _____
   _____

Writing Assignment
Research

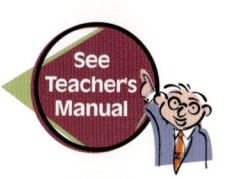

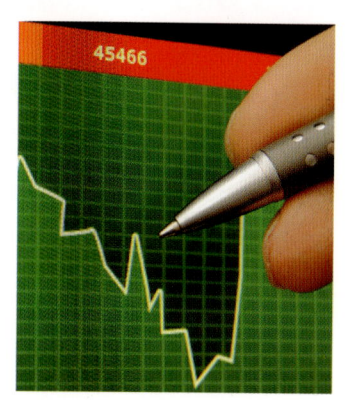

The two most famous polls that exist in the United States today are the Gallup Poll and the Nielsen ratings. The Gallup Poll surveys people's political opinions, and the Nielsen rating system measures people's television-viewing preferences. There are many other polls that measure and evaluate people's opinions on purchases, life goals, and job preferences, to name just a few. Do research on the Internet and find another public opinion poll on a topic of your choice. You may also research about your country's way of evaluating people's opinions on its popular products. Take notes on the kinds of questions that they ask and how the information is presented. Present your findings to the class.

Assessment

Polls and Surveys

Project — See Teacher's Manual

For this project, find out about new trends, issues, or concerns that are important to your classmates and other students in the school, such as the impact of consumption on the environment or the economy, people's buying behavior, or trends in using recycled or reusable products. Then do a survey of their opinions and present your findings to the class. Follow the steps below.

1. Choose a topic.
2. Do research on the Internet about the topic.
3. Create a questionnaire of about three questions to ask your fellow students.
4. Interview ten students to find out their opinions about the topic.
5. Find out the total numbers of how students feel about the issue. Calculate percentages if possible. Explain how.
6. Remember to take into consideration the students' ethnicity, gender, and age.
7. Finally, create visual materials to present your findings to the class.

Your presentation should be structured as follows:
    A. Background or history of topic
    B. Findings with visual aids
    C. Any conclusions based on findings

Grammar Review

ADVERB CLAUSES OF CONTRAST

Adverb clauses of contrast express obvious contrast and unexpected results.

OBVIOUS CONTRAST: While, Whereas

While the smartphone has many applications,	a regular cell phone has only one.
dependent clause	independent clause

"While the smartphone has many applications" is the adverb clause expressing obvious contrast. It is a dependent clause that cannot stand on its own. It must be followed by the independent clause "a regular cell phone has only one."

UNEXPECTED RESULTS: Even though, Although, Though

Doug bought the most expensive phone	**even though** he didn't have any money.
independent clause	dependent clause

"Even though he didn't have any money" is the dependent adverb clause that cannot stand alone without the independent clause.
"Doug bought the most expensive phone" is the independent clause which is also the unexpected result.

The dependent clause can be the first clause in the sentence or the second. When the dependent clause is first, a comma follows the dependent clause. When the independent clause is first in the sentence, no comma is used to separate the clauses.

GLOSSARY

Vocabulary Word	Part of Speech	Pronunciation	Meaning
absolutely	adverb	[ab-s*uh*-**loot**-lee]	definitely, completely, thoroughly
accountability	noun	[*uh*-koun-t*uh*-**bil**-i-tee]	being responsible for someone or some action
agency	noun	[**ey**-j*uh* n-see]	organization, company, bureau that provides some service for people
axis	noun	[**ak**-sis]	in a graph, the horizontal or vertical lines that cross each other
be greeted by	idiom	[be gree did] [bi]	encounter
burst your bubble	idiom	[burst] [yoor] [**buhb**-*uh* l]	ruin your fun
cater to	verb	[**key**-ter] [too]	serve exclusively
charge	verb	[chahrj]	run or rush out
clear as a bell	idiom	[kleer] [az] [a] [bel]	something understood completely and quickly
convince	verb	[kuh *n*-**vin**se]	persuade; make someone believe something
correlation	noun	[kawr-*uh*-**ley**-sh*uh* n]	relation between two or more things
data	noun	[**dey**-t*uh*]	individual facts, statistics, or items of information
dash	verb	[dash]	leave a place quickly because you are late for something
deadline	noun	[**ded**-lahyn]	the time by which something must be finished or submitted; the last date by which a bill must be paid to avoid penalty
dead zone	idiom	[ded zohn]	area where cell phone communication is impossible
detect	verb	[dih-**tekt**]	discover or catch someone doing something secretly; discover the existence of something
detriment	noun	[**de**-tr*uh*-m*uhnt*]	loss, damage, injury, cause a negative impact on something
disclosure	noun	[dih-**skloh**-zher]	showing, revealing, exposing something which is hidden
downside	noun	[**doun**-sahyd]	negative aspect
drawbacks	noun	[**draw**-bak]	disadvantage
ensure	verb	[en-**shur**]	make something definite
file a complaint	idiom	[fahyl] [*uh*] [k*uh* m-**pleynt**]	formally complain about a product, service to a company

financial aid	noun	[fi-**nan**-sh*uh* l] [eyd]	money given by the government to students to pay college tuition
fluctuate	verb	[**fluhk**-choo-yet]	to change continually; shift back and forth
frivolous	adjective	[**friv**-uh-luh s]	lack of seriousness or common sense
get one's money's worth	idiom	[get] [mahy] [**muhn**-eez] [wurth]	receive a benefit from something that is equal or greater than the money you paid for it; get a good quality product in exchange for a higher price.
glance	verb	[glahns]	look quickly at something
go on and on	idiom	[goh] [awn] [*uh*n] [awn]	continue beyond expectation or desire
go well beyond	idiom	[goh] [wel] [bee-**ond**]	exceed expectations
grin	verb	[grin]	smile broadly especially as an indication of pleasure
hold up	phrasal verb	[hold] [uhp]	last for a period of time
horizontal	adjective	[hawr-*uh*-**zon**-tl]	flat or level, parallel to the ground
industry	noun	[in-d*uh*-stree]	companies or fields of business
intercept	verb	[in-ter-**sept**]	to catch, seize or hault; to stop from passing
laundry list	idiom	[**lawn**-dree] [list]	a very long list of things to do
legislation	noun	[lej-is-**ley**-sh*uh* n]	laws made by government
merits	noun	[**mer**-it]	positive aspects
misgivings	noun	[mis-**giv**-ing]	a feeling of doubt, distrust or apprehension
money doesn't grow on trees	idiom	[**muhn**ee] [**duhz**-*uh* nt] [groh] [on] [treez]	you have to work to earn money; it doesn't come easily without effort
neither here nor there	idiom	[**nee**-th*er*] [heer][nor] [*their*]	not relevant; unimportant
on a regular basis	idiom	[awn] [uh] [**reg**-yuh-ler] [**bey**-sis]	happening all the time
originate	verb	[uh-**rij**-*uh*-neyt]	where something comes from
outweigh	verb	[out-**wey**]	be stronger than; have more importance than
overtime	noun	[**oh**-ver-tahym]	work beyond the traditional eight-hour workday that usually pays time and a half
peer	verb	[peer]	to look searchingly; to figure out or understand something
plant	verb	[**plahn**t]	to place firmly in an area
poke	verb	[pohk]	to thrust or push

preferences	noun	[**pref**-r*uh* ns]		the things that one chooses to like more than other things
prudent	adjective	[**proo**-dnt]		careful, cautious
put away	phrasal verb	[poot] [*uh*-**wey**]		save for a late time; save money in a bank account
reflect	verb	[ri-**flekt**]		shows what people think about an issue, problem, or event
regulate	verb	[**reg**-y*uh*-leyt]		control through rules and regulations
relative	adjective	[**rel**-*uh*-tiv]		in comparison to
resigned	adjective	[re-**zahynd**]		accepting of or giving into something you really don't want
response	noun	[ri-**spons**]		answer or reaction
restraint	noun	[ri-**streynt**]		control of one's desires
rubberized	adjective	[**ruhb**-*uh*-rahyzd]		coated with rubber to make it waterproof
scam	noun	[skam]		a plan to trick someone
scheme	noun	[skeem]		strategy; plan
slide	verb	[slaid]		to walk smoothly
soothing	adjective	[**soo**-*th* ing]		calming, reducing of pain or anxiety
testament	noun	[**tes**-t*uh*-m*uh* nt]		tangible proof or tribute; public opinion
toxins	noun	[**tok**-sin]		poisons
trappings	noun	[**trap**-ingz]		attractive features; decorations, accessories
triumphantly	adverb	trhy-**uhm**-*fuh* ntly		behaving in a way that shows that one has achieved success
unfeasible	adjective	[un **fee**-z*uh*-buh l]		not practical or possible
vertical	adjective	[**vur**-ti-k*uh* l]		pointing or standing straight up and down or at a 90 degree angle
warranty	noun	[**wawr**-*uh* n-tee]		written promise by a company to repair or replace a product that breaks within a set period of time
welfare	noun	[**wel**-fair]		physical and/or mental health, happiness; well-being

Source: Dictionary.com

Final Oral Exam

Work with your partner(s). Create a presentation about one of the topics of this book. Be creative and try to use twenty (20) vocabulary words that you have learned from this course and choose one of the following:

Come up with a situation based on the units and create a dialogue.

Give an opinion about the readings and explain your opinion.

Debate issues which are presented in the reading passages.

Practice your presentation. Then, perform in front of the class.

AND REMEMBER, HAVE A GREAT TIME!

TOPICS:

Unit 1. Diversity

Unit 2. Family

Unit 3. Alternative Medicine

Unit 4. Pursuit Of Happiness

Unit 5. Consumerism

Congratulations!

You have finished *Zoni English System, Dynamic Reading.*

Notes